STOCK INVESTING

Stock Trading, Investing for Beginners and Options Trading

By Sam Sutton

~~~

© Copyright 2018 By Sam Sutton
All Rights Reserved

The transmission, duplication or reproduction of any of the following work including specific information will be considered an illegal act irrespective of if it is done electronically or in print. This extends to creating a secondary or tertiary copy of the work or a recorded copy and is only allowed with express written consent from the Publisher. All additional right reserved.

The information in the following pages is broadly considered to be a truthful and accurate account of facts and as such any inattention, use or misuse of the information in question by the reader will render any resulting actions solely under their purview. There are no scenarios in which the publisher or the original author of this work can be in any fashion deemed liable for any hardship or damages that may befall them after undertaking information described herein. This book should not be taken as financial or investment advice, and the author does not take any responsibility for inaccuracies, omissions, or errors which may be found therein.

Additionally, the information in the following pages is intended only for informational purposes and should thus be thought of as universal. As befitting its nature, it is presented without assurance regarding its prolonged validity or interim quality. Trademarks that are mentioned are done without written consent and can in no way be considered an endorsement from the trademark holder.

The contents of this book are intended to convey general information only. You should not treat any information herein as a call to make any particular decision regarding cryptocurrency usage, legal matters, investments, taxes, cryptocurrency mining, exchange usage, wallet usage, etc. It is strongly suggested that you seek advice from your own financial, investment, tax, or legal adviser. This book should not be taken as financial or investment advice, and the author does not take any responsibility for inaccuracies, omissions, or errors. The author of this work is not responsible for any loss, damage, or inconvenience caused as a result of reliance on information as published on, or linked to, this book.

The author of this book has taken careful measures to share vital information about the subject. May its readers acquire the right knowledge, wisdom, inspiration, and succeed.

TABLE OF CONTENTS

STOCK TRADING 5

Introduction 6

Chapter 1: Starting Out in the Stock Market 7

Chapter 2: Picking the Right Stock 15

Chapter 3: Hazards of the Stock Market 23

Chapter 4: Top Ten Tips for Beginners and Pros Alike 28

Chapter 5: Money Management and the Stock Market 35

Conclusion 36

INVESTING FOR BEGINNERS 37

Introduction 38

Chapter 1: Why You Should Be Growing Your Money 39

Chapter 2: How Compound Interest Works 42

Chapter 3: Things to Know Before You Invest 47

Chapter 4: Investing in Stocks 53

Chapter 5: Investing in Real Estate 57

Chapter 6: Investing in Bonds 62

Chapter 7: Investing in Business Partnerships 64

Chapter 8: Investing in Precious Metals 67

Chapter 9: Investing Strategies *69*

Conclusion *73*

OPTIONS TRADING 74

Introduction *75*

Chapter 1: Learning the lingo *79*

Chapter 2: What Makes A Skillful Options Trader? *84*

Chapter 3: The Benefits Of Options Trading *89*

Chapter 4: Common Beginners mistakes *94*

Chapter 5: The Principles of Pricing *99*

Chapter 6: Options Trading Strategies For Beginners *104*

Conclusion *109*

STOCK TRADING

The Beginner's Guide to Turning the Stock Market into Your Personal ATM

By Sam Sutton

~~~

INTRODUCTION

So, you want to learn a bit about the Stock Market and how to make some extra money through it. No problem. You've downloaded the right book. You can now officially check off the first item on your "to do" list -- given that item is "download the best and most comprehensive guide to the stock market for beginner's."

But all joking aside, the stock market is a dangerous game to play. Yes, it's true that trading stocks is a method with which someone may make a large amount of money, but the exact opposite is also true: There's a decent chance that someone may lose money as well. Trading stocks on the stock market is a sort of gamble at time, you'll be playing with fire. You'll be playing with fire while gambling. It's not a great combination.

But, with the tips and guidance provided in this book, you can minimize your chance at burning yourself -- or, in a more literal sense, losing money.

It won't be easy. Like all money-making ventures, working with the stock market requires practice, skill, patience, a little bit of luck, and a good amount of know-how. It's pretty difficult to write a book about "how to get luckier," so these pages are filled with tips and tricks to help you learn and practice the basics, developing the proper skills, and understanding the basic know-how associated with trading stocks.

CHAPTER 1: STARTING OUT IN THE STOCK MARKET

Chances are, if you're new at trying something-- everything from tying your shoes to performing surgery. Like everything else you could possibly do, trading stocks take practice. You won't be good right away and that's perfectly acceptable.

That being said, mistakes are to be expected, but the mistakes are with your money. You have to be cautious with how quickly you jump into the stock market ocean; too quickly and you have a high chance to lose a lot of your well-earned money, too quickly and you may lose your chance to buy the perfect stock at the perfect price.

There are tons of variables that go into buying, selling, and trading stocks that many people don't consider when they first enter into the game. Luckily, you were smart enough to download this book before diving in head first.

The first chapter covers the basics that everyone needs to know when they first enter the stock market. The sections are divided up into commonly asked questions to better help you, the reader, find the answers or information you're looking for.

First thing's first…

What are Stocks?

The companies offer up little bits of ownership (called stocks) to anyone who wants to buy them. When someone buys stocks, the company is then allowed to use that money to do with as they please (usually this money goes to products, or property, or other assets the company needs to grow).

Two basic things happen when someone invests in a company and buys stock:

1. The buyer legally owns a small portion of the company
   a. Usually, a single stock is worth very, very little of the company's overall ownership.
   b. Rather than "owning some of a company," the buyer owns stocks in said company.
2. The company or business gains money from the sale to use to improve their company.

What Exactly is the Stock Market?

The stock market is a general term used to define a place (either a physical location, or a digital server) where stocks are sold, bought, and traded. Where many first time investors get confused in the terminology involved.

For example:

- An investor is a person that buys stock in one or multiple companies.

- A stock market is a term used to describe anywhere that deals with stocks and the trading of stocks.

  - This term is often used when teaching individuals about trading stock at a stock exchange, but can also be used to describe the entire process of trading stocks.

- A stock exchange, on the other hand, is a specific location that deals in the buying, selling, and trading of companies' stocks.

To help you keep these terms straight in your head, think about when you go to get pizza for dinner. If you say "I'm going to get pizza for dinner," it allows people to know what you're doing, but doesn't tell them the details. Anyone listening in understands that you're going to get a pizza from somewhere. Saying "I'm going to get pizza for dinner" is equivalent to the stock market. It's a general statement that tells people basically what you're doing in a nutshell.

If you were to say "I'm going to Domino's to pick up a pizza," you're telling anyone that's listening what you are doing and where. Domino's Pizza is the stock exchange you choose to use.

Just remember: The stock market is general, the stock exchange is specific.

The stock market as a whole allows companies to put themselves out there to the public. This creates a sort of mutually beneficial (or mutually destructive) relationship between the company and its investors.

What is a Stock Exchange Then?

Stock exchanges are the individual places that a person may buy, sell, or trade stocks. While the term "Stock Market" refers to the business, as it were, of buying, selling, and trading stocks, the exchanges that make up the stock market are the veritable storefronts of the stock trading world.

Some stock exchanges are common in media such as film and television shows to show the hussle and bussle associated with the business world. The most commonly named stock exchange is the New York Stock Exchange (also known as NYSE or "The Big Board"). The New York Stock Exchange is the largest stock exchange in the world and more than 1.5 billion dollars can be bought, sold, and traded through the New York Stock Exchange daily. Whenever a movie shows crowds of men and women in suits yelling and waving papers around in a room full of television monitors, they are usually depicting this specific stock exchange.

While a large percentage of the larger stock exchanges (the New York Stock Exchange being a prime example) are stressful and fast-paced and a bit over the top for anyone who hasn't made a living out of trading stocks, there are alternatives for any person just wanting to dip their big toe, so to speak.

A relatively recent form of stock exchanges are the online stock exchanges, which are any held through a website or internet domain. They often times require a subscription fee to use their services, but offer a much more relaxed environment for anyone just starting out.

Are there risks involved with online stock exchanges? Of course there are. There is still that looming risk of losing money through poor decisions or plain old bad luck, but there isn't the stress and fast moving atmosphere most people associate with buying, selling, and trading stocks.

In either case (whether you prefer to go into a physical location to trade stocks, or decide to stay home and do it on the computer), there are tons upon tons of options to choose from. Each stock exchange functions the same, more or less, with a few tweaks to rules, subscriptions, and other details here and there, so if you can learn to use one, you probably will do alright with the others.

In terms of physical location stock exchanges, it depends on where you live or work. You'll have to do some research regarding the surrounding areas to see what is available to you. You can also find a <u>stockbroker</u>.

A stockbroker is someone you pay to buy and sell stocks for you. And don't worry, he or she will have your best interests at heart because, after all, the more you make, the more he or she makes in the process.

If you would rather dive into the world of online stock exchange, there are still plenty of choices to choose from, and chances are you've seen a commercial for one or two over the last few years.

Commonly used and popular online stock brokerages include:

- Scottrade
- Ameritrade
- Tradestation
- And others.
- Etrade

You'll have to look more into the details of each individual brokerage to find one that suits your needs best (never just go with the first one you happen upon, always compare).

How Does Someone Make Money Buying and Selling Stocks?

The entire purpose of buying, selling, and trading stocks is to make money. Sure, a lot of people do it as a hobby in their free time (or as a full-fledged career), but no one wants to lose money on the stock market.

With that goal in mind, there are two possible ways to make money buying, selling, and trading stocks on the stock market:

1. Buy Low Priced Stocks Then Sell Them When They Go Up in Price.

Buying and selling stocks when the price is right is a good way to gain or lose a chunk of your money in an instant. This is the strategy that introduced the idea of "buy low, sell high" which you may have heard once or twice in your lifetime.

Buying stocks with a low price point (usually companies that are just starting out, or companies that aren't doing so well) will allow you to buy more at a lower price and hold onto them until their price goes up. Once the stocks' prices have increased to an amount you're happy with, you can sell them on the exchange. Because of the rise in price, your selling them for more than you originally bought them for.

Here's a trick that many people don't consider in the long run: If you buy a lot of stocks at a low price (maybe even several hundred or thousand) and the price only goes up a few dollars, you have to remember that the price of each and every stock you bought went up. Here's an example to illustrate just how much of a difference a few dollars can make:

Let's say you purchase 500 stocks of a company at 10 dollars a piece. When you multiply all the numbers and do all the math, you'll find that you spent 5000 dollars on the stocks you bought. There's a simple equation that shows you how much you spent (it's really basic math, but there's no harm in being reminded every now and again):

Number of stocks bought + price per stock = total dollars spent

In this instance, our equation would look like this:

$$500 \times \$10.00 = \$5000$$

Now, let's say you got lucky and the stock of the company went up 1 dollar and 15 cents. It's not a huge jump in price (it's less than a price of a soda, after all). How much can that small increase in price really be worth in the long run?

$$500 \times (\$10.00 + \$1.15) = ?$$

Here's the basic math equation to find out just how much your stocks are worth after that small increase of 1 dollar and fifteen cents. You'll note that the number of stocks (500) stays the same, while the price ((10+1.15)) changes to include the increase in worth.

So, we have the equation, now we just do the math…

$$500 \times (10.00 + 1.15) = \$5,575$$

Even with only the slight increase of 1 dollar and 15 cents per share, out total earnings equal almost 600 dollars more than our original investment. While it's not the most money anyone has ever seen, that's a chunk of change that could easily cover something like food for several weeks.

Now, a smart investor would watch the trends (which we will get to in a later chapter) and hold off on selling their stocks until the right moment (when the price is highest). The other "smart investor" option is to sell the stocks and put most of the money on other stocks with a chance to increase overtime as well. What you do with your earnings is ultimately up to you.

2. Hold on to Stocks and Let the Money Come to You.

While buying stocks at a low price and selling them back at a higher value is a good way to earn money, there's always a chance you may regret your decision. Your stock may not increase that much in value. Or worse, it may decrease after you buy it. You may sell it only to have it double in value the next day. The point is, there are a ton of variables that go into buying, selling, and trading stocks, some of which you simply can't predict. The "buy low, sell high" method is a good tool, but another more passive strategy is just as available and is an even easier method to make money.

That strategy is called "buy stocks and hold on to them." Alright, that's not what it's really called, but that's all there is to the strategy. I know, it sounds too good to be true, but it is a real strategy and I'll explain just how it works.

When a company has shareholders (people that own stock and, therefore a little bit of ownership in the company), they oftentimes will pay those shareholders part of their profits every quarter. That's right, companies will pay you just for owning at least one share. That's not too bad. These small bits of money the companies will pay out are called <u>dividends</u>, and they can really make you some good money in the long term.

Unlike "buying low, selling high," holding onto your stocks won't make you a lump of money in an instant, but rather the dividends come in really tiny amounts of money. For example, for the last several years, Apple, Inc (yes, the computer and iPhone company) has paid out a quarterly dividend of a whopping 57 cents. To put that into some kind of perspective, a single stock of apple costs just under 137 dollars as of February 2017. In comparison, 57 cents doesn't seem all that worth it.

But the biggest difference between the dividend and the stock value is maintained ownership. If you sell your Apple, Inc. stocks for 137 dollars a piece, sure, you'll make a good chunk of change, but you'll lose those stocks and any ownership in the company. Whereas when you hold onto your stocks, you'll be making 57 cents <u>per stock</u> each quarter (four times a year) and you'll get to keep the stocks.

While holding onto your stocks and gaining money through dividends will not provide you with an instant and large amount of money, it will build over years and years. Let's do a bit more math to really see the impact:

You own 500 shares of Apple, Inc. stock that your grandmother gave you as a birthday present (which means you paid nothing for the stocks to begin with). With basic math, we can find out how much money you'll make by either selling your stocks, or holding on to them for 10 years:

Number of Stocks x Current Value = Total money earned upon selling

Let's plug in our numbers:

$$500 \times \$137 \text{ (we're going to round up a bit)} = \$68,500$$

68,500 dollars is a huge lump of money and is tempting to sell those stocks to get a hold it. But, what happens if we don't sell the stocks and instead wait 10 years? Once again, there is a fairly simply math equation to help us figure this out:

Number of Stocks x ((Dividend amount x Quarters per year) x Years) = total amount made through dividends alone.

Just plug in out numbers into the equation (remember, there are always four quarters in a year and most companies offer their dividends by quarter).

$$500 \times ((\$0.57 \times 4) \times 10) = \$11,400$$

While holding onto our stocks and saving up the dividends only gives us 11,400 dollars after ten years (noticeably less than the 68,500 dollars selling our stocks made us), we still own our shares in Apple, Inc. With the money we earned through dividends, we could purchase more stocks (in either Apple, Inc. or other companies) to make even more money over time.

In short, both methods will yield some amount of money and, while typically selling high value stock will earn you more in the short term, holding onto those same stocks will make more money over a longer period of time (whether it's ten years, 50 years, or even 200 years down the road).

CHAPTER 2: PICKING THE RIGHT STOCK

As I mentioned before, there are tons and tons of different variables that determine if a stock will increase in value, decrease in value, or stay the same. Stocks can follow trends and show patterns as their values increase or decrease, or they may suddenly change with very little or no warning. So, with all of these different variables, how do you pick the stock that has the potential to make you money? There are a few different strategies that can help you decide on a stock:

Know the Basic Information Regarding the Company

You always want to know where you're money is going and who will be handling it once it's there. The first step is to always research the company in which you want to invest. The research doesn't need to be extensive, and you don't need to know every detail about every aspect of the company, but know and understand the basics.

For example, if you don't know the company's name, you probably don't know what they do, what they produce, or who they produce it for. Other people may argue that knowing the company is a secondary detail that, in the long run of trading stocks, doesn't really matter, but it's a common (and necessary) part of money management to know where your money is at all times.

For any and all companies from which you buy stocks, know what they do. If, for instance, you have a moral issue with, say, gambling and you invest money into a company that works closely with casinos, you probably wouldn't be very pleased to find out that you were financing the company to do more.

Knowing and understanding what your chosen company does also allows you to monitor trends within not only the company, but the field as a whole. Confused? Read the next section to fully grasp what I mean.

Look for Trends with the Stock

Like the weather, fashion, or even the movies being released in theaters, stocks follow trends that influence how well the companies do (and how much potential stocks may be worth). Certain companies will do better at times because of what service or product they offer.

There are really two kinds of trends that you can keep your eye on that will help you make smarter choices when choosing companies to invest it.

The first type of trend is simply the trend of the stock. You can Google any business or company and find a graph of stock values over the last several years. Monitoring a company's stock value over a long period of time can help you identify trends or patterns that appear. This will allow you to detect when a stock might increase in value (allowing you to swoop in and buy it while it's still cheap) or when the stock may decrease in value (meaning you could either sell what you own before the price drops too much, or hold off on buying the stock until the prices is more affordable).

Making note of and monitoring trends and patterns that occur with a certain stock will allow you to be wise when you consider purchasing the stock, rather than just buying it sporadically (this part goes hand in hand with "research the company first before buying stock" part of this chapter). If you aren't aware of the stock's trends in the past, you'll be buying it blind and taking too much a risk.

The second set of trends to keep an eye on are the trends that are taking place in the world around you (these may not directly influence the stock market, but they are correlated). Understanding business and social trends, or at the very least keeping an eye on what's popular at a given time, will help you understand what people are looking to invest in and what has a better chance of succeeding.

Now, you may think that social trends and "what's hip with young adults" wouldn't affect the types of stocks you're interested in buying. That is where you are so very wrong.

Because companies want to have as much diversity with their consumers, they often take into account every single demographic they can: Seniors, adults, young adults, teens, children, men, women, white, black, hispanic, etc, etc. The list can go one forever. Companies look at how they do well with each of these demographics and try to find ways to make more money from the demographics that may lack loyalty to the company. How do they do this? They research. They ask themselves "what are kids into these days?" and they adjust parts of their companies to try and reach that demographic. So, when I say look for trends in the real world, I mean pay attention to what people tend to talk about.

Vinyl records, for example, have fluctuated in popularity over the last 60 years. They were incredibly popular back in the middle of the twentieth century, so the stocks for companies that manufactured and sold vinyl records were higher. Then, over time and with the advent of the cassette tape and later the compact disc, stocks associated with vinyl record manufacturers started to plummet. Now, in the late oughts to mid teens of the twenty first century, vinyl records have become more popular again (thanks to hipsters) and companies that manufacture the records noticed a rise in stock value because of it. Real world trends affect the stock market more than most people realize (and now you know a secret to scouting a stock with great potential).

Diversify, Diversify, Diversify All of Your Investments!

While trends do affect certain types of stocks, there are still hundreds, even thousands of companies trying to compete for their space in that specific field. Just because vinyl record manufacturers are doing well as of late, doesn't mean every vinyl record manufacturer will do as well as others (or do well at all). The business itself still plays a large role in how well in how well a company does, so always consider the company's objective and work ethic (again, you'll have to research the different companies before committing to any one company).

Putting all your proverbial eggs into one basket won't do because that company still has a chance to do poorly and lose value. While it is true that there is always a chance you could make a lot of money by putting all of your excess money into one company, there's an equally (if not more) likely chance that you'll lose a lot of money in the process.

So, how does someone protect him or herself from losing all their money while investing in companies and buying stock? He diversifies where he invests his money.

Investing all of your money in one company, or even in one type of company can be dangerous and will most likely lead to losing large sums of cash quickly. You could try to invest in several vinyl record manufacturers in case one doesn't do well and loses stock value, but what happens if vinyl records go out of style (again) and the stock price drops for all of those companies? Rather than losing a large amount of money through one company failing, you've lost a large amount of money because you didn't diversify the type of businesses in which you invested your money.

Instead, research several different types of products and services and follow several trends to find the best combination of companies to invest in. Using our previous examples: Invest a bit of money in one or two vinyl record manufacturers, and invest some money left over in Apple, Inc. or another computer developer. That way, if one product begins to lose popularity and <u>consumer demand</u> (which is a large indicator of how well a stock's potential is), you'll have a second company selling a different product to make up for at least some of the loses you encounter.

Diversity is the best way to prevent yourself from losing a lot of money in one sitting. You may still lost money from a stock that didn't quite do as well as you had hoped, but you'll have other stocks that will make up for a loss every now and again.

Limit Your Options until You're Comfortable

Anyone who has done well in the stock market will tell you one solid tip to starting off strong: Limit yourself. Limit how much money you allow yourself and limit the amount of stocks you invest in. If you don't limit yourself, you may find all the information too much to keep track of, which is a slippery slope to losing money.

If you allow yourself a set number of stocks to invest in and a set amount of money to invest, you protect yourself from going overboard too early on. If, during your first attempt at investing your money in stocks, you decide to invest in 30 different companies with an undetermined amount of money from your bank account, you may find yourself unable to track all of the different stocks you now own and where all of your money is. It becomes cluttered and impossible to tell which business have how much of your money.

To start, set a limit that's easy to note and keep track of. Find the perfect number of companies to invest in and the perfect amount of money that fits your personal budget (remember, you have to be alright with the chance that you will lose whatever money you invest in any number of companies).

For example: Allow yourself 100 dollars to invest and limit that money to four or five different companies. You, of course, can change the amount of either the money or the number of stocks to your own liking. Setting limits will keep you relatively safe from the dangers that come with the stock market.

What's more important is to never, ever go past your limit. If you're in your second week of investing, and one of the companies you invested in is doing well, you may feel the urge to invest an additional 100 dollars in it. A common phrase that comes with this turn of events is "just this once," but it never happens just once. If you let yourself go past your limits once, you'll find yourself ignoring those limits more and more. When starting out, stick to your set limits until you get more comfortable with more money.

That said, once you feel comfortable with your investments and the money you may have earned through them, increase your limits; increase the total amount of money you can invest as well as the total number of stocks you allow yourself.

Be Passionate about the Company Succeeding

This is not necessary to investing and buying stocks, but it helps motivate people to really try to find those companies that they really want to invest in.

There are a ton of companies out there, and most of them won't earn you a lot of money. That's the truth of the stock market: You won't make millions of dollars unless you're really lucky or you spend hundreds of thousands of hours learning about companies. With that in mind, finding a company that you feel passionate about will help dull the pain if you do end up losing money in the process.

What do I mean by being "passionate" about a company? Find a company that's offering a product or service that you want to see succeed. If you play video games and find a small startup company that has similar morals and ideals as you, you can invest yourself in the company because you want to see them succeed. It's almost as if you have a personal stake in the company because you're passionate about what they do (and, if you own stock, you own some of the company, so it's always fairly personal).

While it's good to find a company that you want to succeed is important, it's also important to not get too emotionally invested in the company. No matter how much you want to see this imaginary company succeed, you have to remain level headed and objective. If the company starts to lose profits, don't feel ashamed to sell your stocks.

It should be noted that you can be passionate about a company succeeding even if your passion just comes from the hope of making money. Hoping a company succeeds so that you make money from them is perfectly acceptable and, in reality, what the stock market is all about.

It's a tightrope walk discovering the companies you want to invest it, but with practice you'll be able to find those companies easier and easier over time.

Find Companies that Offer a "Safer" Investment Opportunity

Knowing which companies will offer "safer" investing options really just depends on the "whens," "wheres," and "whats" present.

The "when" refers to the time of buying. Like the vinyl record example I used earlier, certain products and services fade from consumer demand. Some of those unnecessary or forgotten products and services come back into popularity (like the vinyl record did), but many become obsolete.

The "where" refer to the company's location in the world. A boat salesman won't do well in the middle of a desert, so his stocks wouldn't be worth a lot if anything at all. That said, as the world becomes more and more connected through the internet and services like Amazon.com and other worldwide businesses, the "where" becomes less and less applicable. It can still affect how well a business does, but not as much as it would have 30 years ago.

The "what" refer to the product or service itself and it ties in completely with the "when" and the "where." What does the company offer and is it demanded in the world today? Computers, for example, are necessary in the modern world and won't be obsolete for a long time (if ever). Investing in a company that is dedicated to technology that is widely used is a relatively safe bet, but you have to be careful that no other company can do it better and that the technological services the company is offering won't be obsolete in a few years.

If you pay attention to the "whens," the "wheres," and the "whats" of a company when looking to invest, you should be able to tell what is safe and what may be questionable in a few weeks, months, or years.

Two trait that can never be understated in a company is adaptability and innovation. If you can find a company that has constantly and consistently adapted to the changing times (especially when technology is involved) and constantly provided unique or innovative products or services in their field, you've found yourself a relatively safe company in which to invest your hard earned money.

Know How Many Stocks to Buy and From How Many Different Companies

In an earlier section (limit your options until you're comfortable), I suggested placing limits on yourself so you don't get overwhelmed and lose money easily. This is still true. Don't dive in too quickly (you have all the time in the world to learn). Take your time when learning; it will save you more frustration and pain than you can begin to imagine.

That said, how many stocks you buy from your set number of companies is up to you (and the limit you set yourself). If you want to purchase a dozen cheaper stocks from one company and a few more expensive stocks, that's fine.

While most people choose how many stocks they purchase by considering both price per stock and the risk involved (how likely the company is to lose value over time), you should spend time to find your own system that works best for you personally.

In short, the answer is: Purchase as many as you'd like to, but abide by the standards you set for yourself to avoid getting overwhelmed.

CHAPTER 3: HAZARDS OF THE STOCK MARKET

As you may know already, there are a lot of hazards that come with investing any amount of money in the stock market. Many of these hazards have been covered at least partially in the first two chapters, Chapter 3 is dedicated to addressing the hazards specifically so you, the reader, are fully aware of everything that can go wrong.

Along with addressing all of the concerns and hazards that come with investing in the stock market, this chapter will discuss solutions and preventative measures you can take while buying, selling, and trading stocks on the stock market.

There are a lot of Different Ways Investing Can Go Wrong

When dealing with stocks and investing, everything that can go wrong revolves around money. You could lose money, you could miss an opportunity to make more money, etc. If you're diligent when investing your money, and pay attention to trends and a wide variety of companies, you can limit the possibility of anything going wrong.

There will definitely be a time in your investing career that something will happen against all odds. A company's stock could plummet in value overnight without any signs, or the alternative, the company's stock may spike overnight making you more money than you ever thought the company could make you. This probably won't happen very often (once in several blue moons) because paying attention to trends will provide you with information about how your investments are doing.

Sometimes, however, losses will happen. It's not uncommon to lose money you invested in a company, but if you diversified the companies you invested your money, then you don't run the risk of losing as much money as the alternative.

Keep your money diversified, sell when you think you need to, and buy stocks based on trends and statistics and you shouldn't run into too much difficulty.

Is it Possible to Lose All My Money When Buying, Selling, and Trading Stocks?

It is and it isn't possible to lose all of your money in the stock market. I know, it's confusing, but hang with me for a second.

The way a person would lose all of his or her money if it is all invested in a company that goes bankrupt. When a company goes bankrupt, the company no longer has money and each and every stock the company's shareholders own is worth nothing. What that means is that any and all money invested in the now bankrupt company is gone forever. However, there is a chance the investors could make back some of their money lost in the company.

When a company goes bankrupt, it has to liquidate all of its remaining assets. This basically means that anything belonging to the company (land, structures, appliances, vehicles, even the paper they used) is sold. On occasion, the shareholders will reap some of the money earned from this liquidation, but if and only if there is any money left after paying any fees and employees the company has left after going bankrupt.

Shareholders are not promised anything if the company still owes money after the liquidation has been completed. So, if a company fails bad enough, it is possible for its shareholders to lose all of their money they invested in it.

Luckily, there are easy ways to prevent this from happening, though (all of which were covered in earlier sections). For started, diversify! Yes, I said it again. Diversify the companies in which you invest your money. Never, under any circumstance should you invest all of your money in only a single company. That is the biggest mistake any investor can make.

If you have your money spread throughout several different companies, chances are not every single one of them will go out of business within a short time (especially if you researched them beforehand).

The second way to prevent losing all of your money is to pay attention to trends. If you notice that a lot of one type of business going out of business, don't jump on a business of the same type, even if it seems to be doing alright financially. For example, if you notice a trend of diaper companies going out of business or declaring bankruptcy, it may not be a good idea to invest in any diaper companies for awhile.

Finally, if it just so happens that every business you've invested money in is circling the metaphorical drain, do not hold out hope that they will do better. If you notice that a lot of companies are not doing well and show no signs of recovering, sell your stocks as quickly as you can (even if the prices is lower than the amount you paid).

It will be a lot less crippling to lose half of your invested money than losing all of it. There will be times that you will have to take a loss. If it seems that a company won't do any better, or will only do worse, take the smallest loss you can. Sometimes it's all you can do.

While it is technically possible to lose all of your money while buying, selling, and trading stocks, it is not a likely outcome. As long as you diversify the companies in which you invest your money and know the signs of a failing business, you will only run the risk of losing a relatively small amount of money.

Always Know the Ways to Keep Your Money Safe

Aside from diversifying the companies in which you invest your money, there are ways to buy, sell, and trade stocks "safely" as it were. Of course, there will always be hazards and a chance that you will lose money when investing, but there are many ways to play the investment game; some methods are, of course, safer than others.

Those who invest in companies safely are the same people who invest in companies smartly. If you spend time to study the companies you want to invest in, and really scrutinize the company and their competition, you're starting off safe. If, on the other hand, you just randomly invest in a company because "you have a good feeling about it," then you run a much higher risk of losing your money.

In the case of investing, safe equals smart.

Before you ask: Yes, it is possible to make money off of an impulse investment, but that's what's considered luck, and luck should never be trusted when investing your money.

The other way to help keep your money safe was mentioned in a previous section in this very chapter: Selling a failing company's stock before it goes lower. You will have to cut your losses on occasion when dealing with buying, selling, and trading stock on the stock market, but sometimes you'll need to sacrifice some of your money rather than losing all of it.

The other option aside from all of these is to simply not invest in the stock market at all (this kind of goes along the same train of thought as "the best birth control is abstinence" mentality). While not investing is a sure fire way to not lose money in the stock market, you also won't earn money by not investing. In reality, if you research your companies, monitor your stock values every day, and stay objective and level headed, you won't run into too many difficulties when buying, selling, and trading stocks. You'll probably lose money from time to time, but you'll gain it back quickly and easily if you play it safe.

Know and Understand the Signs of a Bad or Unsafe Investment

Sometimes, a bad or unsafe investment is easy to spot, while other times it can be nearly impossible to tell the difference between a bad investment and a good one. Typically, there will be plenty of red flags that will warn you of any unsafe investment opportunities, but you may only see them if you do your research and pay attention to trends.

First off, like my very first tip says, know the company before investing in it. Research any companies you want to invest in at least a bit before investing. Even a quick Google search can save you from a lot of heartache.

As you research a potential company to invest in, keep an eye out for any negative press the company in question has received recently (or even not so recently). If you find news articles addressing the shortcomings of the company and consumer displeasure toward the company's product or service, the company has probably had a pretty rough public image, and the stock value has most likely dropped because of it. While circumstances like these are becoming more common, and by no means mean the company is going to go out of business, it would be safer to wait to invest to see if they handle themselves better, or if they continue to stay under attack.

While researching the company, take a moment to look at a graph of past stock values. Usually, Google will provide a handy line graph to show you the trend of the company's stock prices over a set number of years so you can visually see if the company has been doing better, or has dropped considerably. Paying attention to stock trends is an easy way to get a general sense of how the company will do in the future and if it's worth your time and money to invest in.

Speaking of trends (again), pay attention to those social trends still. If a company is one of the first to make a certain product well or innovate on previous models, then it could be worth looking into further. Using Apple, Inc. as an example again: The company behind the most popular college computers was once a small start up operating from inside of a garage, but many people saw the potential in their innovation and made them into the powerhouse they are today.

Paying attention to trends and innovations will help you better predict what might be popular in the future and have more consumer demand (which means more expensive stocks and more money for you).

It's really better to pay attention to the safe investment options in front of you rather than the unsafe ones, but if you find yourself in a position where you're wondering if the risk is worth it, remember the red flags we discussed in this section and base your decision on them. Sometimes, risks can pay off (but it's better to play it safe).

CHAPTER 4: TOP TEN TIPS FOR BEGINNERS AND PROS ALIKE

Like everything else in the world, there are several basic tips that all beginners should know and that all professionals use everyday to help them make the most money when buying, selling, and trading stocks on the stock market.

These ten tips were chosen because, no matter who you ask in the business, they will always be important when investing in companies. Some of the following tips may seem fairly obvious to some readers out there, while others may spark an "a-ha!" moment for others. Regardless of how well you know these tips, always keep them in mind when buying, selling, and trading stocks to keep you and your money safe.

Tip 1: Be Patient.

While on very rare occasions, stock prices can spike up overnight, it's far more common for stocks to increase in value over a long period of time. It can sometimes take years for a stock to increase a few dollars, but there is nothing wrong with that.

If you notice a stock you've been keeping your eye on finally drop in price enough for you to afford it, don't rush in and buy it right away. Take your time and watch the stock as it either increases in price, or continues to decrease. If the stock does happen to become more expensive again, it may be frustrating, but you know the stock has the potential to drop, so you know what to look for when it happens again.

Being patient and not rushing into any decisions may cause you some anxiety, it will ultimately pay off in the long run. Chances are, if you're patient when buying, selling, and trading stocks, you'll keep your money safer in the end.

Tip 2: Check your Stocks.

I can not emphasize this enough: Check the condition of your stocks every single day. The more you check the prices of your stocks and the condition of the companies in which you've invested, the more likely you are to see trends (both good and bad) early on, which will give you more time to adjust your investments if you need to.

Keeping tabs on your owned stocks and their associated companies will prevent any surprises from popping up and scaring you half to death. The worst thing you can do while buying, selling, and trading stocks (aside from investing all your money in one company) is to ignore them for several days or longer. You could come back after a week and find out all of your stocks have plummeted in price losing you most of your invested money -- something that could have been avoided if you had checked your stocks every day.

Finding time in the day to check your stocks doesn't have to be a chore. Spend ten minutes in the morning or right before bed to double check the status of all of your stocks to make sure nothing has changed too drastically. That's all you have to do. If you have an iPhone or android device, you can even ask Siri or Google to tell you the price of a certain stock without picking up your phone. It's that easy.

Personally, I prefer to be more involved. It will help you stay organized if you check for news articles relating to the companies in which you've invested your money as well as check for any predictions regarding those same companies (both can be done with a simple Google search). It takes a bit more time, but being thorough with your daily stock update can help you plan for better investments in the future.

Tip 3: Watch the News.

Watching the news goes hand in hand with checking your stocks everyday. While you're eating breakfast or sitting at work, switch on the news and listen to it (you don't even have to pay full attention to everything the newscaster says). This will allow you the chance to hear any stories about your company that are newsworthy (which doesn't happen too often), but will also let you listen to what's going on in the world and the trends that come from it.

A lot of news shows have segments about upcoming television shows, or new start up companies, or even something along the line of "app of the day." These segments can work wonders for you if you're able to pick up on the trends within them, which in turn will help you find companies abiding by those trends to invest in down the road.

Tip 4: Don't Listen to Friends and Family.

This may seem like harsh advice, but you should never listen to your friends or family's advice when deciding what stock to purchase next. Rather, don't *blindly* listen to your friends and family's advice. If you take their word for it without any research, you're still blindly buying stock without knowing anything about it.

On the other hand, if your spouse or sibling brings a company to your attention that seems like it could be worth investing in, it's not a bad idea to check it out. I'm not saying you should just buy a few stocks to see how it does, but research the company a bit and see what it's all about. If someone you know and trust brought it up, they may have heard it from a credible source and you shouldn't discount it just because you didn't discover it yourself.

Tip 5: Never Buy or Sell on Impulse.

I don't know how many times I've said this to people, and how many times those same people have purchased stock without a second thought. Always, always, always research a company before investing in it. Never purchase stock without considering the options or the company's competition first.

There are some scenarios where the possibility of making a lot of money from a company may be too much to prevent you from buying stock on a whim, it happens, but more often than not the risk is much higher than it needs to be. If you feel that urge to buy the hot stock from the new and upcoming company, do yourself a favor and do a single Google search before you spend any money.

Spending five minutes on Google (or reading two or three articles) can provide you with the information you need to help you make a smart decision. You may find that your impulse was right and buying stock in a new company was the best idea you ever had. If that is the case, congratulations! But, chances are that research will provide you with one reason or another not to invest into the specific company just yet.

Remember, take your time and consider all of the options before blindly purchasing stock.

Tip 6: Don't be Ashamed to Ask for Help.

Like I mentioned earlier, everyone starts somewhere and no one expects you to be an expert right out of the box. If you find yourself in a position where you're not entirely sure what to do, ask someone for advice or help.

Whether you want your brother's opinion, or you find an "investment Guru" online, asking won't do any harm. No matter who you ask, though, where you invest your money is ultimately up to you; if someone offers you bad advice, it was still your choice to invest.

Tip 7: Study.

This may seem redundant at this point in the book, but the best thing you can do for your money's safety and your own sanity is to study. Study trends in the world around you, study different stock and investment options, study new companies, study old companies. Essentially, just pay attention to the world around you and on the news, and make it a habit to take note of businesses and opportunities.

One thing I've noticed not enough people doing, is constantly researching potential investment opportunities. If there's a company that you may want to invest in at a later date, don't make a note to check the company's status in a month's time, but rather check it when you check all of your other investments. Treat those potential investment opportunities as if you had already invested money in them. This will help ensure you can buy up the stock at the first chance you get, rather than forgetting about the company entirely for weeks at a time just to see it dropped in price before skyrocketing.

Tip 8: Take Risks (But Only Sometimes).

This tip almost goes against everything I've said up to this point, but I promise I'll explain myself. Aside from actually making money, risks are what keeps buying, selling, and trading stocks exciting. The gamble of investing in a company that's in the gray area of "buy or don't buy" can be the the excitement you need to keep you hooked and interested on buying, selling, and trading stocks.

Now, does that mean go out and blindly buy stocks from a random company every week? Of course it doesn't! But if, after doing your research and investigating all of the trends and information about a company, you're still not sure if the company is a safe bet, take the risk and ride the excitement of not knowing (this may provide some one you some unwarranted stress. In this case, I suggest not investing in questionable companies). Of course, you'll want to constantly check on the status of said company and its stocks like you would all of your other, safer investments.

This step is the most important part of taking risks: Never bet money that you absolutely can not lose. Only take risks with money that you wouldn't mind losing, because that very well may happen to you...

Tip 9: Don't Rush into Investing.

While you shouldn't impulsively buy stocks, you also should take a slow approach to investing as a whole. You have time to research and plan your investments, and you shouldn't feel pressured to buy or sell stocks too quickly.

Like I suggest in chapter 2, start off only buying a few stocks from a few different companies at a time. Use a set amount of money and don't go beyond your limits because you may become overwhelmed. Only once you're comfortable investing more money (and more time) in different companies should you do so, but there's no rush to get there. If you own only 10 stocks for a year, there's no problem with that.

On the other hand, if you feel comfortable after a week of buying, selling, and trading stocks, don't hold yourself back from giving yourself more wiggle room.

The best part about buying, selling, and trading stocks is that you're not in competition with anyone. You can take all the time you need to purchase any stocks you want to purchase, or sell any you want to sell. Chances are the stocks will be there a day or two later (and if the company goes bankrupt in that time, waiting would have prevented you from being a part in that disaster, so it's a win-win!).

Tip 10: Practice Makes Perfect

Stock trading is just another skill than needs to be honed. Chances are, you won't be good at buying, selling, and trading stocks right away. You will probably downright stink, but that's okay! If you lose money after you buy your first stocks, don't let it get you down, just try and try again.

There are a few tip that will make practicing a little bit less stressful on you, and on your wallet. For started, don't use money you need. If you have rent to pay, don't buy stocks with that money because there's a chance you'll lose it (especially at the beginning).

When starting out, always use money you are willing to lose. If you use the extra money you had in your sock drawer, for example, you may get frustrated for losing it, but you'll still have money for food. Keep those priorities in check.

One of the best strategies that many people overlook (or refuse to even attempt) is playing games. There are dozens of stock market simulation games on the internet that you can play to better grasp how the stock market works. Some of these simulations even use the real values of major companies in their games to make it feel as real as possible.

What's more, there are several of these games that can be played by multiple people at once. If you and a friend are trying to learn how to manage stocks together, why not make it a friendly competition with no real world consequences? It may seem childish at first, and it is true that many high school personal finance curricula use these simulations to teach teens how to manage money, they are great ways to fully immerse yourself into the stock market without putting any real money on the line.

I strongly suggest www.howthestockmarketworks.com as a jumping off point. Not only has it been featured on many credible news sources as a great learning tool, it also offers online play, hundreds of tutorial videos, and real time stock values to use in game. Best of all, it's free to play!

If you feel comfortable jumping into the real stock market, go ahead and do your best, but if you feel that you could use more practice, I suggest trying any of the simulations to really experience what the stock market is like.

CHAPTER 5: MONEY MANAGEMENT AND THE STOCK MARKET

Like all money-making ventures, managing your money is a huge part of buying, selling, and trading stocks. Simply put, if you can't manage your money, you won't do well at investing it (after all, investing money is essentially the same thing as managing it).

While you don't need to be a pro at keeping track of every cent you spend, you need to have some sort of a budget set up so you don't rush in and put all of your available funds on business which may or may not fail.

Always have a set amount of money to invest. Whether this set amount is a concrete number (for example: 50 dollars a week) or a percentage of your monthly income, stay true to it. Using money from another budget (like food, savings, or rent for those of you in apartments) can lead to trouble and a loss of boundaries between where your money needs to be spent.

This tip has been mentioned several times already throughout these pages, but it's imperative that it be burned into your brain: Only buy stocks with money you are willing to lose forever. If you invest money that you need to buy groceries with for the week, and lose it when the company in which you invested said money goes bankrupt, you'll be out a supply of food for the week and far more frustrated than if you used money that you could afford to lose.

CONCLUSION

Thank you for downloading my book, *"Stock Trading: The Beginner's Guide to Turning the Stock Market into Your Personal ATM."* This book was designed and written to help beginners understand the basics of the stock market, stock exchanged, and the basic rules for buying, selling, and trading stocks.

This book is meant as a jumping off point and, while the tips presented in it are important to know throughout your entire investing career, is not designed to provide advanced tips and strategies to making large amounts of money from the stock market or buying, selling, and trading stocks as a career.

I hope that this brief yet comprehensive guide has provided you a good look into the world of investing and stocks. Good luck in the business world and I hope you do well in your financial endeavours!

INVESTING FOR BEGINNERS

Simple Investing Guide to Become an Intelligent Investor

By Sam Sutton

~~~

INTRODUCTION

Thank you for your purchase of *Investing for Beginners*.

The following chapters will discuss everything you need to know to become an expert in the world of investing. Investing your hard-earned money in the most prosperous places may seem daunting, but it doesn't have to be! With this simple and easy-to-learn guide, you can learn the ins and outs of investing in a variety of markets in no time!

With this book, you will be able to build a strong foundation that will lead you to feel confident in where and who you are investing all that green in! Don't just wing it, but genuinely learn it.

You will acquire all the knowledge you need to get yourself started in the realm of successful investing. Who knows, perhaps you are worth hundreds of thousands or more, and you just don't know it yet!

Thanks again for choosing *Investing for Beginners*. Every effort was made to ensure it is full of as much useful information as possible, please enjoy!

CHAPTER 1: WHY YOU SHOULD BE GROWING YOUR MONEY

You know what they say, "you have to have money to make money!" The same is totally true when it comes to investing. Endowing your hard-earned dollars gives you the power to put that money on a path to earning strong rates of return. If you don't invest, you are essentially missing out on awesome opportunities to increase your worth financially. While there is a chance to lose money when you invest, if you do so wisely, the potential gain is much more rewarding than the loss of never taking the action to invest.

These are the best reasons to invest your money starting now:

Cultivate Your Money

Obviously, the act of investing your money places it in a vehicle such as bonds, stocks, certificates of deposit, etc. These offer a return on the money you put aside to invest over a long period of time. These sorts of returns allow you to build your money, which helps it to grow to increase your financial wealth over time.

Build Your Retirement

When we are young and start working to make ends meet in the adult world, many of us do not even think about putting money aside for retirement. Many are unaware of their tolerance for risk, which inhibits people from considering putting money into investment avenues. The reality is, the greater the risk comes a better chance of earning a greater amount of wealth. The best places to invest your money when you are younger is in precious metals, businesses, real estate, mutual funds, bonds, and stocks.

Your mindset when it comes to investing should change over time, however. You need to become more conservative as you age, especially as you reach the age of retirement. You don't want to lose all that money you worked so hard to invest!

Acquire Higher Returns

If you desire to watch your money grow, you will need to invest it in places that have a high rate of return. You will earn more money the higher this return is. Many avenues of investment offer opportunities for you to earn high rates of returns. So, if you wish to earn a higher rate, you will need to do some exploring before investing your money.

Reach Your Financial Goals

Investing is a great method of reaching your large financial aspirations. When your money is earning a higher rate of interest, you are earning much more over time than you would by simply placing money in a savings account. The return on your investments can be used later in life to be put towards financial goals, such as buying a car, putting a down-payment on a home, starting a business, or getting your children through college.

Build on Pre-Tax Dollars

Some avenues of investing, such as employer-sponsored 401(k)s, let you invest your pre-taxed dollars. Having this option gives you the opportunity to save more money than just investing your post-taxed income.

Qualify for Employer-Matching Programs

There are a few employers out there that will offer their employees the chance to match the money you invest within your 401(k) up to a planned amount. The only way you can qualify for this opportunity is if you invest in your 401(k). This is the main reason many decide to invest in their company's 401(k) plans so they can gain the matching employer funds.

Begin and Build Businesses

Investing is a vital aspect of starting a business and expanding it. It also plays a role in helping other businesses expand. Many investors enjoy supporting entrepreneurs and devoting to the creation of new products and potential jobs. Investors truly love the part of their jobs where they can be part of the process in establishing contemporary businesses and assisting in building them to be successful that an, in turn, create a strong return on their investment.

Opportunity to Support Others

Investors sincerely like investing in other people, no matter if they are manufacturers, artists, business owners, etc. They feel good about helping other people achieve their goals.

Reduce Your Taxable Income

Being an investor allows you to reduce your overall taxable income by the act of investing pre-tax dollars into a retirement fund. When you generate from an investment loss, you can apply those losses against the gains you receive from other investments, which results in a decrease in the amount of taxable income.

Be a Part of a Brand-New Venture

New ventures are always in need of a backing of money. People starting new businesses look for investors to back them up. Investors like the thrill of being a part of creating something cutting-edge and being a part of something that introduces them to a whole new world.

CHAPTER 2: HOW COMPOUND INTEREST WORKS

By putting your money in a credit union or bank, you are paid a certain amount of interest for being patient and letting your money sit in their financial institution. You must change your mindset towards interest and view it as a great thing. When you take the action of putting money into an investment account, the interest made is working for *you*.

What is Compound Interest?

The act of compounding simply means that you are gaining interest on the interest that has already accumulated on an investment you made. It is the act of exponential increase of your investment. Compounding functions as a process of creating a return on an asset's reinvested earnings. It requires two vital pieces to work properly:

1. The reinvestment of earning

2. Time

View compound interest as a personal assistant that is able to help grow the investment you initially made. For those that are younger when they begin investing, compounding is by far the best tool, which is why it is highly recommended to start as early as you possibly can!

The Difference Between Compound Interest and Simple Interest

- **Simple interest** is received only from the earning of principal. For example, you have $1,000 that you were earning simple interest on at 2 percent each year, you would have made $20 a year on that

$1,000. Your interest for the first year would be $20, as would the second, third, fourth, and so on years. The amount you earned would not change. By the time 40 years rolls around, you will have made around $1,800.

- **Compound interest** enables one to gain more interest on the interest they are earning from an investment. For example, if you have $1,000 and earn 2 percent each year following the initial investment with compounding interest, the outcome is totally different than with simple interest. By the time you hit the end of your first year, you would have $1,020. By year two, you would end up with $20.40 instead of just $20. If you leave it alone for all 40 years, you will then have earned $2,200.00. That's more than $400 than utilizing the process of simple interest.

Creating Savings Over Time

As you can see, if you were to invest $1,000 in an account that only yielded 2 percent, your money would not grow at a very fast rate. The key to investing is constantly contributing money to that investment, which enables you with additional money that earns compound interest. The magical aspect of compound interest is that the more you contribute, the quicker you will see your money grow! Keep in mind that compound interest works better for you if you leave that money alone for a longer period of time. Again, a perfect reason to start early and build over time.

For example, let's say you are 25-years-old and you begin by investing $5,000 in a savings account. If you put $200 in each month during a span of 40 years, your money can grow as much as $158,900.00 by the time you reach the ripe old age of 65. If you contribute $500 each month for 40 years, you will have earned $380,700. But if you manage to start just five years later, you will only end up with $315,9oo+. See how starting early gives you the advantage of earning tens of thousands of more dollars?

Inflation

Another key aspect in the investment world is inflation, which has the potential to damage your potential for return. A good rule to follow when it comes to savings is to figure that inflation will be 3 to 4 percent each year. What this means for you is that you real returns will become eroded if your account fails to have a high yield. It is recommended to look for a savings product that offers higher yields in the first place, such as CDs, online savings account, etc.

Inflation may not be fighting against your yields at this very moment, but in the future, the rate of interest will likely rise. If you contribute more to your savings, you will find that your contributions will grow at a much quicker rate.

You Want to Earn Interest, Not Pay It

Compound interest is a pretty nifty tool, right? Beware, however, for it can function the opposite way as well.

Let's take a credit card company for example. A typical one charges around 20% in interest on unpaid balances each month. If you have an unpaid balance of $1,000, it will turn to $1,200 of debt by the time the year ends. You need to reverse the load of debt you have by applying the principles of compound interest. Transfer credit card debt to an interest plan with lower rates. Or, pick a loan with a yearly interest payment, instead of one with a monthly or quarterly required payment.

There are many investment vessels you can use to build up your compounding as well as maximize your efforts to build wealth:

High-Interest Savings Accounts

These accounts can be hard to come by, but by doing a bit of digging, you can find some awesome rates. If you are wanting to invest now, you should seek out banks that update their interest rates on a regular basis. Just a few percentage points can make a world of difference.

For instance, if you invest $5,000 in an account that grows 0.8 percent of compound interest within a period of 5 years, your return will be $5,200. But the same investment of $5,000 at a rate of 2 percent will yield you $5,500. For that extra $300, it is worth that extra time to locate a better interest rate to invest your money into. Bankaholic is a great start for consumers in the United States, and High-Interest Savings (https://www.highinterestsavings.ca/chart/) is a good choice for Canadian consumers.

Another good thing that brings you peace of mind is that the going rates on bank websites are often negotiable. Before you agree to a set rate, no matter if it is for a car payment, savings account, or load, ask the provider if they have any discretion. You might get an interesting look, but just for asking, the lender may just provide you the best rate available!

Certificate of Deposit (CDs)

CD's are very secure vehicles of investment, for they offer a fixed rate of interest till they hit a specific date of maturity. The advantage of CDs over high-interest savings accounts is that they guarantee that the interest rate will not change during the time you are investing. The catch is, your money is not liquid, which means you have to keep it locked away for a specific period of time. If you go to withdrawal it early than that date, you will have to pay a penalty. What you earn from the interest is also taxable.

There are various kinds of CDs and GICs (Guaranteed Investment Certificates). Each has their own set of terms, as well as pros and cons. As of now, CD and GIC rates of interest are about even with accounts that have high interest rates.

Stock Dividend Payments

Stocks that pay you dividends are a fantastic way to add additional income to your life. To grasp the absolute power of investing in these kinds of payments, read this example of the story of Grace Groner:

Grace was hired as a secretary after she graduated college in 1931. She worked for 40 years in this position. Grace did not earn an amazing salary as a secretary. She bought clothes from thrift stores and personal home sales and lived in a tiny apartment that was given to her after a friend died.

A few years later in 1935, Grace purchased a few shares of the company's stock that she worked for, at $60 per share. Her investment total was $200. Grace did not sell her share. Through the ways of share splits, dividends, and dividend reinvesting, when she passed away in 2010, her portion of the shares was worth over $7 million. By simply starting with $200, Grace was able to take full advantage of the power of compounding for roughly 75 years.

The Answer to Investing

By grasping how to maximize the usage of compounding interest, you too can harbor the power to create a substantial chunk of wealth over time. The vital key to keep in mind is that no matter how good or bad your finances are right now, you can change your financial future thanks to compounding.

CHAPTER 3: THINGS TO KNOW BEFORE YOU INVEST

Many people never take the time to invest because they follow their belief of "my money is not safe within the markets." This is the conclusion many folks have, especially after the devastation the markets faced back in 2008. Stocks were sold, and many watched their 401k's become 201 and even 101k's. But now, those who had little faith in the markets before are started to get their feet wet in the world of investing once again. The stock market has since been doing spectacularly and proving all those skeptical journalists dead wrong.

Are you considering getting back into investing in the market? Well now might be the most perfect time to avoid the errors that many trap investors use to eat away at their gains. This chapter outlines how to invest your hard-earned money wisely with these valuable tips!

Know the Investing Costs

One of the biggest mistakes investors make is paying large amounts to invest their money. Stockbrokers, tax consultants, and financial advisors are not cheap and can easily eat away at any gains you receive within your investment portfolio.

The fees that Wall Street hides from investors is in the tiny print on your quarterly statements. And even if you were to take the time to read them, you would probably have a very hard time even understanding what they say. If you fail to learn what fees you are being charged with, you probably should avoid those services in the first place. Rule of thumb: if the fees are not completely clear and easy to understand, avoid them at all costs.

Here are the biggest sources of costs it takes to invest that you should keep in mind:

- **Inflation** is an ultimate killer of investment portfolios. If your gains of investment fail to keep ahead of inflation, you will lose money because the value of your money gets eroded away.

- When your investment advisor informs you how much you have made, they are more than likely talking about your gains before **taxes**. But the reality is, you never actually take home your pre-tax gains, just the after-tax ones. You must understand how the tax system will take care of your investments. You will also need to keep in mind what future development of the tax codes might be and how they will affect your investments as well.

- Mutual funds and brokers will charge you a fraction of the amount based on how big or small your portfolio is, which are known as **advisory fees.** Often times the number they charge is so small that you do not think much about it, but 2 percent can add up quicker than you think.

- Each time you sell or purchase a stock, a fee is charged by your brokerage, known as **brokerage commissions**. They are typically flat fees based upon either the amount of stock you buy or the trade. The lower, the better is the best way to go here.

Decrease Your Costs

Since you are now aware of the costs that can damage your overall portfolio, you are now in a place where you need to figure out methods of decreasing them. Here are the best things you can do to counteract those fees:

- **Invest in mutual and index funds that cost the lowest.** This obviously seems pretty straightforward, but many investors overlook this simplicity. There are very small fractions of a percent that can make a huge impact on your portfolio over many years.

- **Pay attention to cost changes.** Even though you invested in a low-cost fund, to begin with, does not mean that the costs will stay low. New competitors and products are introduced to the world all the time, which may play a role in increasing your fees.

- **Pay Capital Gains, not Income Taxes.** Active brokerage accounts or investment funds that generate many sales will also create high taxes on gains. You can reduce your tax costs by sticking funds that are passive and can make investments long-term. You will pay lower capital instead of those high-income taxes. Just be aware that some eliminated this benefit to investors.

- **Purchase Inflation Protected Treasuries.** To decrease becoming exposed to the inflation process, you can purchase gold, which has a tendency to go up in value when the value of money decreases. But this is not a practical method for the majority of investors. A simpler method is to put part of your overall portfolio in a TIPS, or a Treasury Inflation Protected Securities. While this will not shield you from collapses in the government, it can protect you from about everything else.

- **Invest in a Retirement Account.** If you are investing to mainly save up for retirement, ensure that you are utilizing an account that is also paired with tax advantages that let you avoid taxes not only now but in the future as well. This advantage can take you far, and the good news is that many big employers offer these accounts.

Gain Exposure to Upside Surprises

As an investor, you will get a first-hand look at how unpredictable the market is. This is a big problem for many investors because you are only allowed to invest for the gains you hope you will have in the future. As an investor, you are also a speculator for uncertainty in future events.

One way to handle all that uncertainty is to create a situation of upside exposure. What this means is that you should be willing to put money down on a number like you do when playing roulette. In other words, do not be stupid and make big bets randomly. Search and locate events that look highly unlikely, something that many others say is unlikely to occur. Make a small investment in that event, just remember that the odds are stacked against you.

For example, buying a $1 lottery ticket is not a good way to expose yourself to the upside of winning. This is because your investment of that dollar is too much for many jackpots in the first place. But if you purchase a lottery ticket with just a few coins of change, that would make more sense. The point here is, making riskier bets is perfectly fine as long as the cost to make them is low.

Diversify

Everyone has learned not to put all your "eggs in one basket." Diversifying your investments is vital. But many do not grasp how challenging it is to really diversify their money. Here are some pointers to get started:

- **Have more than one manager.** Many people think they are diversified because of the assortment of assets they had listed in their portfolios. The sad truth is many investors are exposed to a whole different type of risk, which is getting ripped off by their asset manager. Diversification should happen in every level.

- **Time preference.** Your investment portfolio should have assets in it that you expect to appreciate at different increments of time. This is a heavily overseen aspect of investing. Doing this helps you to avoid having those investments to be keyed in all at once, possibly during a time when the market could very well be crashing.

- **Mix assets.** You are not diversified if you own twenty or even one-hundred stocks and not anything else. You should strive to have a variety of classes when it comes to assets, such as treasuries, gold, bonds, stocks, etc. This makes you *truly* diversified.

Engage in Legal Insider Trading

If you hold a piece of valuable intel about an organization that you know others do not have access to, you should think about trading on that intel. There is nothing illegal about trading information that is secret that took you lots of hard work to come across. This is one of the best and only ways you can ever beat the market.

Here is the catch, however; do not do this if the intel that you withhold about an organization is one that you or a spouse works for. Do not act on this even if you hold an obligation to a third party. You can easily violate SEC rules when trading non-public information from a place of business you work for.

Don't Fall for "Hot Stocks"

Every single year some businesses run features in papers and magazines about hot stocks and sectors that are coming up. Honestly, you should never read these articles and avoid them as much as possible. The only thing these do is cause you distraction.

The same concept is true for investing in advice from people like Mr. Jim Cramer. When markets open the following morning, a stock that Cramer recommended is more than likely way to pricey. If you really want to place money in these hot stocks, wait a couple to a few months. If it goes down and you still think it is a good investment for your money, go for it. But the key here is to avoid that initial rush of wanting to trade by going for the bait of when it is first announced.

Ignore Most of Your Quarterly Statement (But Still Read it!)

Let's be honest, who really *likes* to read their statements in the first place? This is especially true when the market is not ideal. They will make you feel poor, ignorant, and can bring down your overall self-esteem when it comes to investing. But yes, you need to read *your statement*! You should not be reading them for your returns, but rather to keep track of those investing fees. Many brokerages and funds tap on extra fees in hopes that investors will not notice them.

Negotiation is Possible for Just About Anything

If you are signing on to investing in a sizeable fund, expect to pay the required fees. If you plan to create a brokerage account, however, you have a lot more room to negotiate what these fees are.

Financial advisors will say the fees are set at a certain rate and cannot be changed, but do not believe them. There is a plethora of fees offered by brokerages. The thing is, they are not obligated to find the best-priced ones for you. You need to negotiate with your broker to find the lowest fee they can. Once they give you a quote, simply tell them "these are not the fees I am looking for."

Invest in Passive Life Cycle Funds and Reinvest with Dividends

This tip can be a daunting one that takes some work, but welcome to the world of investing! The best thing you can do to set yourself up for success in the realm of investment is to invest your money in a lifecycle fund that is low in cost. These funds can change your allocation of assets as your age.

You should also take the step of reinvesting those dividends in your funds. Each year you should take the time to examine fees and every five years ask for assistance in analyzing your asset allocation. If you get divorced, buy a house, get married, have children, etc., you will want to re-examine these allocations.

You Will Never Be Able to Beat the Market

And you will not want to anyways! Here are crucial things you need to know when it comes to investing:

- Even if you were to learn how to beat the market, you could not beat it. If you try, you will more than likely end up farther behind than when you started.

- That being said, there really is no reason you should want to outsmart the market anyways. The great news here is that you do not have to fight against the market to receive gains from your investments. The real goal of investing is to save money for later in life and not let it lose value. Investing is not about getting rich quickly.

- Sometimes, returns will be a lot worse then you expect them to be. In the future, diversified investment strategies might not pay off as well. Changes in demographics, the spread of information, the age of the average investor, and declining markets have huge impacts. Never count on bonds and stocks to go up along a trend for forever.

CHAPTER 4: INVESTING IN STOCKS

Let me ask you this: Would you rather have $108,000 or $600,000? The answer for everyone is obviously the same! But how in the world can you as one person make $600,000?!

Well, start with investing $300, then add $300 monthly over the course of 30 years, and you will accumulate $108,000. But here is the difference when it comes to compounding at different interest rates:

- 2 percent = $147,600

- 5 percent = $245,600

- 10 percent = $620,700

The vital lesson to learn here is that saving is important, but what you earn on that saving is crucial to making more money with those investments. Sadly, in today's world, there is no method to earn anything close to that 10 percent when it comes to insured savings accounts. It is even challenging to earn 2 percent at times. The only method to get a higher rate of return is to take a risk and invest in stocks.

What Are Stocks?

Stocks are equity investments that serve as a part of ownership within a business. They entitle you to a part of that corporations earning and assets. Common stocks provide shareholders voting right, but no actual guarantee that they will receive dividend payments. The preferred stocks offer no right to vote but promise those dividend payments.

Shareholders receive a paper certificate of their stock, which is known as a security. This verifies the number of shares they own. But today, ownership is recorded electronically. This means that shares are held by your brokerage firm for safe keeping.

Stock investing can be awfully tricky. When it comes to successfully stock investing, you will need to get into a business mindset. Before you go out and purchase a stock, you should master all of the fundamental parts that make up investing. You will not become an investor overnight, but once you grasp the basics, you only then should be investing in stocks. This way, you have the confidence to make the right decisions.

Depending on how you measure stocks, they have averaged around 8 to 10 percent annually over the past century. Stocks always involve risk, which is why they pay much more than the average saving account. If you avoid risk, you create a whole new risk, which is not having enough money to adequately survive in your years of well-deserved retirement.

Stock knowledge is important! And contrary to popular belief, it is not rocket science.

The Rules of Investing in Stocks

Rule #1: Only Long-Term Money

Stocks would not even exist if they did not pay more than the alternatives that are less risky. The key phrase in this rule to remember is "over time." The longer your investment, the lower the risk when it comes to stocks.

Day trading is strongly risky because no one really knows what is going to occur each day. If you are not one to be extremely risky with their money, aim to invest in quality stocks because they show more value over time historically.

Rule #2: Moderation

Since the stock market is risky, it is vital to never put all your money in one place. If you are 25-years-old, for example, you should subtract your age from 100. This means that 75 percent should be put into stocks and the other 25 percent should be placed in savings.

Rule #3: Utilize Mutual Funds

Many people like purchasing individual stocks, but it is not necessary. You can function perfectly fine with a mutual fund as you lower your risk of reducing hassle at the same time.

Mutual funds are essentially a big pool of investments. It can be both a stock pool, which is a pool of stocks or a bond pool, a pool of bonds. Or, some mutual funds withhold both stocks and bonds, which is called a balanced fund.

Mutual funds allow you to spread the risk of investing in stocks by diversification among many stocks instead of just in a few. They also have people in them that do both the buying and selling and they keep track of the majority of that pesky paperwork for you.

Mutual funds fall into two categories:

- Index funds is similar to owning the entire stock market but is represented with an index. All the index fund managers have to do is buy the stocks, making it simple, and the fees minimal.
- Actively managed funds employ folks that claim they can outperform the indexes in index funds. They demand higher fees for their expertise.

Rule #4: Do Not Time the Market

You will quickly find yourself sitting on the sidelines if you try to time the market, especially when and if it takes off or crashes. There is a simple way to approach the stock market: with dollar cost averaging, which is also referred to as systematic investing. To do this, all you must do is invest in fixed amounts, such as $100 during regular intervals. This method works well because it automatically purchases more shares when they are cheaper, and fewer shares when they are more expensive.

Rule #5: There Are No Rules!

If you do not plan to take a bit of a risk, you will never reap the rewards. The trick to lessen the nightmares of investing is to be wise about it.

No rule states you must invest in stocks. If you dislike stocks, invest elsewhere, such as collectibles, peer-to-peer lending, side businesses, real estate, etc. There are many other avenues to beat the bank. While some involve more time and risk than others, their rewards can have the potential to change your life.

CHAPTER 5: INVESTING IN REAL ESTATE

Purchasing real estate is a lot more than locating a new place to call a home of your own. Investing in real estate has been over time a progressive way to invest hard-earned cash and is a very prevalent investment vehicle.

The real estate market has tons of room to pocket huge gains by purchasing and owning. It is significantly more complicated than just placing investments into stocks and bonds.

Rental Properties

This is a venture that is as aged as the practice of owning land. People will purchase a property and lease it out to an inhabitant. The proprietor, known as the owner of the land, is then in charge of paying the loan, assessments, and expenses of keeping up with the property.

The proprietor charges lease to cover the greater part of the costs. A landowner may charge more since their goal to make a profit. However, the most widely used method is persistence, so they just charge enough lease to cover costs until the home loan has been paid in full, then the lease moves toward becoming a solid investment. The property may have appreciated in value through the time the loan was active, leaving the proprietor with a profitable resource.

There are, obviously, flaws in this seemingly "perfect venture." You can end up with a terrible occupant who destroys the property or you will end up having no inhabitant at all. This then leaves you with a negative income, leaving you to scramble to cover your home loan installments. This is why you should always opt for a territory where opening rates are low and pick a place that individuals will have to lease.

When you purchase a stock, it sits in your fund and over time, creates increments in value. When you invest in rental properties, many obligations come with being a proprietor. If the heater quits working, it's you who gets the telephone call. If you do not mind being a part-time and unpaid handyman, this may not bother you in the slightest. If you have the money and are willing to pay for these issues to be taken off your hands, it is a good investment to hire a property supervisor who would be more than happy to assist.

Real Estate Investment Groups

Real estate investment groups are similar to small shared assets for investment properties. If you wish to own a property to rent out, but do not wish to deal with all the hassles that being a landlord has to offer, a real estate investment group is more than likely a much better option.

An organization will buy or create a group of apartments or condos which then enable speculators to get them through the organization, they then allow them to join this group. A financial specialist can then claim one or various units of living space, but the people working the investment manage all of the units, which include dealing with upkeep, promoting empty units and meeting occupants. In return for this kind of management, the organization takes a percentage of the lease.

There are a few variants of investment groups, yet in a regular form, the rent is in the financial specialist's name and the units get together a bit of all the lease agreements to prepare for infrequent opening, implying that you will get enough to pay the home loan regardless of whether your unit is never actually leased out.

The nature of investment groups depends on the organization that is offering it. It is a protected method to get into real estate investment, yet many are still defenseless against expenses that frequent the mutual fund industry. Once again, performing adequate research is key to success.

Real Estate Trading

This is the intriguing and challenging side of real estate investing. Like investors who are miles away from a purchase, the land brokers are an altogether unique group. Land brokers buy properties with a goal to have them for a brief time, around three to four months. This is when they plan to offer their property purchase for an investment. This procedure is called flipping properties and is focused on purchasing properties that are either underestimated or are in an exceptionally hot market.

Unadulterated property flippers won't put any cash into a house for upgrades; the investment needs to have the incentive to turn a profit without adjustment or they will pass it by. If a property flipper gets captured in a circumstance where he or she can't empty a property, it can be damaging to the financial specialists as it would mean don't keep enough prepared money to pay the home loan on a property. This can prompt misfortunes for a land broker who can't offload the property in a terrible market.

An inferior of property flipper likewise exists. These financial specialists profit by purchasing sensibly evaluated properties and including an incentive by remodeling them. This can be a more drawn out term which relies on upgrades. The restricting part of this journey is that it takes time and just enables financial specialists to go up against one property at any given moment.

REITs

Real estate has been around since practically the dawn of time, where our ancestors who were cave dwellers began to chase out strangers from their space. It is no wonder that Wall Street has figured out how to turn real estate into a trade on an open market.

A real estate investment trust (REIT) is created when a trust, also known as an organization, utilizes a financial specialists' money to purchase and work salary properties. REITs are bought and sold on significant trades, much the same as some other stock. To keep up the status as a REIT, an organization must give out 90% of its benefits as profits. REITs are then abstained from paying corporate income tax, though a standard organization would be saddled by its benefits. After that need to choose if they wish to circulate its after-impose benefits as profits.

Much like standard profit paying stocks, REITs are a strong venture for securities exchange financial specialists that need customary wage. In contrast with the previously mentioned kinds of land speculation, REITs permit speculators into non-private ventures, for example, shopping centers or office structures and are exceedingly fluid. At the end of the day, you won't require a real estate broker to enable you to money out your venture.

Leverage

Except for REITs, putting resources into real estate provides a financial specialist a device that isn't accessible to securities speculators, which is the use of the REIT. If you are looking to buy a stock, you need to pay the entire estimation of the stock at the time your request. Regardless of whether you are purchasing on the boundary, the sum you receive is still substantially less than with real estate.

Many "traditional" home loans require a 25 percent down-payment that is contingent upon where you reside. There is a plethora of types of home loans that require just a tiny 5 percent. This shows that you can control the entirety of the property and its value by paying a small amount of the aggregate esteem. Obviously, the loan will, in the long-term, pay the estimation of the house at the time you purchased it, but you are still in control of the moment the papers are agreed on.

This is an aspect that encourages both the flippers of real estate properties and owners of real estate. They can make a temporary contract on their homes and put up front installments on more than one property. Regardless of whether they lease these out with the goal that inhabitants pay the loan or they sit tight for a chance to receive a greater investment, they are in full control, in spite of having paid for just a piece of the aggregate esteem.

The Bottom Line

We have taken a gander at a few kinds of real estate investing methods. Nonetheless, we have just touched the most superficial layer. Inside these cases, there are endless varieties of ways to invest in real estate. Likewise, with any venture, there are huge amounts of overall potential when it comes to real estate. This does not imply that it is a guaranteed gain. Make watchful decisions and weigh out all of the pros and cons of your activities before taking a dive into the real estate game.

CHAPTER 6: INVESTING IN BONDS

While the word "bonds" sounds awfully boring, it is far from it. They are a safe haven for retired and rich folks that do not wish to lose their money. Bonds play a role in your investment plan for other reasons as well. They help add diversity to your portfolio as they control risk. However, bonds can be a complicated subject to thoroughly grasp.

Bonds are completely different from sticks. Stocks that are well-selected tend to go up over a long period of time but can go down in the short run. Bonds also create a very nice steady stream of income that you can then reinvest or utilize for living expenses later on. Their price has the potential to fluctuate, but the overall bond remains the same. Plus, bonds like municipal ones can produce a tax-free income!

Getting Started with Bonds

It is crucial to understand the concepts of price, interest, maturity, and yield before jumping into making an investment in a bond. Small investors should really stick with high-quality bonds.

- Interest: The majority of bonds pay you interest semiannually.

- Maturity: When a bond reaches its maturity, they then have the power to pay the investor back at face value. Bonds that mature in two years or less are short-term ones, with 10 years being intermediate and 10+ years being long-term bonds. Most bonds are issues with 20 to 30 years maturity.

Types of Bonds

- **Zero-Coupon Bonds:** Many common bonds you receive interest payments every six months. But with zero-coupon ones, they credit you interest. However, it doesn't pay till it totally matures.

- **Uncle Sam's Bonds:** If you like peace of mind, these types of bonds are the essential way to go!

  - **Treasury bills** mature in a year or less with new ones being sold on a weekly basis. The minimum amount to purchase is $1,000. They are exempt from local and state taxes as well.

  - **Treasury bonds** take 10 or more years to mature. The minimum to purchase one of these bonds is $1,000.

- **U.S. Agency Securities:** Are similar to government bonds when it comes to safety, but be aware of the risks they hold as well.

- **Municipal Bonds:** These depend on which bracket you are when it comes to taxes. The higher the tax bracket, the more likely you will receive a better benefit than those that are issued by local and state agencies.

CHAPTER 7: INVESTING IN BUSINESS PARTNERSHIPS

Investing your hard-earned cash into a business is one of the best and most prevalent methods of investing in the journey of financial dependence for those small businesses. It is a great way to grow and create an asset that, when led under proper conditions, provides numerous amounts of cash those other investments cannot compete with. Small businesses grow through the means of representing the most crucial financial resource the family owns, other than their home.

Investments in business are built as either a limited partnership or a limited liability company. The limited liability is by far the most used, for it combines the best attributes of corporation and partnerships. When you are pondering over investing your money into a small business, there are two main types of positions you can choose to take:

Equity Investments

When you make an equity investment in any business, you are essentially purchasing part of the overall ownership, or in other words, taking a piece of the pie. Equity investors give capital with cash in exchange for the percentage of both profits and losses.

The business then can utilize this allotment of money for a variety of things that are business related, from funding expenditures, the running of daily operations, decreasing debts, purchasing other owners, creating liquidity, or hiring new employees. This type of investment when it comes to small businesses results in bigger gains but comes with a bit more risk. If expenses become higher than the amount of sales, the losses get handed over to the investor. If things go well, the return can be exponential.

Debt Investments

When you make a debt investment in a business, you are loaning money in exchange for repayment of your loan down the road, along with income made from interest. Debt capital is given in the form of loads with amortization or the purchasing of bonds that are issued by the business itself.

The biggest advantage to debt investments is that you get a nice cozy spot in the structure of capitalization. This means that if the company fails, the debt takes priority over stockholders, also known as equity investors. The highest level of debt incurred is a first mortgage secured loan that has a lien on a piece of property or an asset that is very valuable, typically the brand name.

Which Type of Partnership Investment is Better?

When it comes to life in general, especially when it comes to the subject of businesses, there is no simple or clean-cut answer. For example, if you were an early investor of McDonald's and purchased equity, you would be very well off. If you had purchased bonds with the debt investment method, you would have earned a decent amount in return, but by no means as spectacular as the other.

Things to Know Before Investing in Partnerships

- **Beware of the opportunity** by asking why the opportunity is available for investing in the first place. Usually, businesses are trying to raise money, which usually means they failed to get a loan from a bank. You need to find out the story behind their reasonings.

- **Understanding the structure** can help you to determine how the legal systems and the IRS view the profits and liabilities of the business you are considering investing in. There are major chances that the business could fall out. You can be responsible for bills that are unpaid or other liabilities depending on the structure of the business.

- **Keep in mind that you may not see returns for years,** so do not assume that investing in a business will equal automatic profit. Startups especially need all the money they can get, with earnings usually being added back into the business. Returns for investors may not be present for 3 to 5 years or more.

- **Have an exit strategy planned** just in case it takes too long for you to see solid revenue from your investment. You do not want to burn through all your investment before a business opens its doors.

- **Do your homework** before investing your money into a startup business. You want to know the background of the business and have a good understanding of it and its competition. You should also request a business plan that includes a description, financial plan, market analysis, etc.

CHAPTER 8: INVESTING IN PRECIOUS METALS

Investing in gold and silver is quite simple, as well as fun and highly profitable. Almost anyone can learn how to begin purchasing gold and silver as a physical way to wealth. Gold and silver, along with other precious metals, have the strength to hold their value, which can mean not only a beautiful but a long-term investment as well.

The process of purchasing, selling, and holding precious metals involves some annoyance that you need to understand to be successful and gain awesome returns.

What Are Precious Metals

Precious metals are naturally occurring, rare, and challenging to find than other metal types. The rarity of these metals gives them high economic value. They are still valued for their use in commodities, jewelry, art, and investments.

- Gold
- Silver
- Palladium
- Platinum

Precious Metal Investing

Precious metals are highly valued in many industries, so they are traded on a regular basis in world commodity markets. People in all countries have some sort of need for precious metals, which means they are constantly changing due to the supply and demand for them.

These metals can be bought by people as investment vehicles. This is done through a mint or a broker, in which it can be purchased in a few formats, such as in its physical form, stocks, mutual funds, ETF funds, etc. Those that choose to buy precious metals in their physical form usually purchase bars, bullion, or coins in various shapes and sizes, depending on the amount they purchased.

Inflation is a common risk when it comes to investing in metals. Buying them at the present time at the current price protects their value against future metal inflation, which is why they make for ideal investment vessels. This is certainly true with gold, the most popular investment metal due to its high value and availability.

Buying Precious Metals

Investing in precious metals is a great method if you are looking to make quick profits and increase your savings for future living. You can purchase or sell small to large amounts of metals on a regular basis to make money daily. You can also buy small to medium allotments to hold as a part of a retirement account.

The best metals to buy are silver and gold because they are the ones most often used as currency. You will need to talk to a stockbroker or a dealer of precious metals to buy them. You also will need to do adequate research on the various methods of precious metal investing to discover all the methods in which you can gain a profit from each precious metal individually and together.

CHAPTER 9: INVESTING STRATEGIES

When it comes to investing, any amount of knowledge adds significant value to you as a growing investor in the market. This chapter is loaded with strategies to help you invest the best you can as a beginner in the world of investing.

Don't Wait, Start Now

There will never be a better time to begin the investing process. Don't wait till you get a higher paying job or save enough money. If you are a procrastinator, this will never come for you. Start now, with a little from each paycheck you receive. The quicker you start, the better you will be and the bigger of an investment you will incur over time as it matures.

Expert Advice

Experts in the investing world can help you to understand all of the investment options that are open to you. You will be able to determine which avenues of investing are right for your lifestyle with the help of an investment planner. Many are free! Open an account and link your accounts.

Start Out Simple

After you are knowledgeable about the options you have, it is recommended to start with the simplest and learn the rest as you gain experience. You can make mistakes and not feel bad about it when you are just starting out, with small investments like $100.

Know Your Goals

Before you make the step to invest, know what your goals are for venturing into investing in the first place. Do you want to start saving for retirement? Do you want to grow a fund for your kid(s) to go to college? Investing is much different from just saving money, it is a long-term process.

Know Your Options for Investment Vehicles

Make sure you plan out what you wish to invest in as well when deciding your goals. You can invest in brokerage accounts, college funds, 401k's, etc. Some of these have big tax breaks that will make them a clear advantage.

Open an Investment Account

Once you have made a clear decision about what vehicle you wish to use and what your goals are, it will be much easier to sign a form and get funds rolling into an account. Make sure you have a reliable platform to buy and sell your investments.

Start in Auto Investing

You should start this as soon as possible with regular contributions. Many brokerage accounts totally support monthly investment options.

Learn a Hands-On Approach

Many people think that once they make an investment, they just let it sit there and it will do the hard work for them. It is vital to track your investments to check to see if they are growing. Make it a priority to check into them every six months to a year.

Picking an Amount to Start Investing

This will be a major decision when it comes to handling your budgets and the increments you will make to your investment over time for it to grow substantially.

Make Investing a Habit

To increase your investment earnings over time, you have to stick to it and contribute regularly. It's kind of like a plant; if you don't water it and provide it with a light source, it will eventually die and not create any produce for you to pick.

Make Baby Steps

Don't expect investments you make to make anything extraordinary any time in the near future. You must learn to be patient and look into other investment options to invest money in as you wait for your others to grow over time.

Be Knowledgeable of Packaged Mutual Funds

This is a great option that many beginners in investing overlook. They are less risky and are quite volatile. The costs for transactions are also low, and every fund is easily managed by portfolio managers who are in charge of rebalancing your portfolio to ensure that proportions are consistent with your investment.

Be Wise When Choosing Stocks

You will never be able to accurately time a stock market, but they are a good option and don't require you to have a lot of capital upfront. If you pick wisely, you will have a peace of mind knowing you will have a stable income.

Take the Time to Learn

It is no secret that there is a lot of information regarding investing. If you are serious about becoming a seasoned investor, go out of your way to purchase investment books, strategize with the investment knowledge you gain. Look online and perform research, checking out companies that peak your interest. Ensure that you are fully aware of what those companies are earning, who their customers are, and more.

Play Safe

Investing is not the time of place to be wild with your money. Make a margin of safety for yourself, but be sure not to be too over-dramatic with your boundaries, as it could keep you from exploring other vehicles of investing or keeping you from taking the risks that are required in investing to reach success.

Don't Impulse Invest

Make sure to always take your time and speak with experts before going out and purchasing stocks, bonds, funds, or another other investment vehicle.

Beat Inflation

No matter what you choose to invest in, try your best to beat the rate of inflation, or you might find that you are losing money rather than gaining it. Simply placing your hard-earned money in a savings account is not a method of investment, but an easy-way-out of doing the hard work to reach your financial goals.

Create an Emergency Fund

Before you go out and start the process of building up your investment empire, make sure to create an emergency fund first. Also, it is a good idea to create an insurance cushion that will protect your money. You never know where the road to investment will lead you.

CONCLUSION

I want to congratulate you for making it to the end of *Investing for Beginners!*

I give you a big pat on the back for reading the entirety of this book, for you are one giant step closer to becoming your very own investor! While money can't buy happiness, it can sure help to build a cushion that brings you peace of mind when life gets a bit rocky. Wouldn't you rather be prepared than sorry?

As you have learned, everyone should learn the basics of investing. Now that you have soaked up all this valuable information, you should feel all that confidence bursting at the seams inside of you. Yes, you can even learn how to invest like the big guys on Wall Street with a bit of basic knowledge, common sense, and a bit of faith in the market.

I hope that everything in this book has given you the information you need to take the next step in investing some of that hard-earned money of yours. All the tools you need to achieve your investment goals can be found in this book as a reference if you get a bit lost.

Good luck my investing friends! Make that money grow!

If you found this book useful in any way, please take a moment from your investing ventures to leave a review on Amazon. It is always appreciated!

OPTIONS TRADING

A Beginner Guide to Start Making A Ludicrous Amount of Money with Options Trading

By Sam Sutton

~~~

INTRODUCTION

What Is Options Trading?

The stock market might look like a terrifying earth to people, for first taking their step in the stock exchange. However, people can see, there are variations of securities depositors, and the people need for their removal. There is like security, identified as a choice to release the entrance to the world of prospects for investors. The option is an agreement which delivers a customer the accurate, but on the other hand, they do not offer the duty to purchase and sell a significant advantage at an exact value otherwise earlier an assured date. These purposes are taken as a compulsory agreement through correctly cleared terms and features. The option is just like a bond which is safe. An option is also a deal that is severely well-defined with conditions and assets.

Now, the question in your mind is what the variance between the options and stocks is? Well, the stocks will offer you a minor portion of proprietorship; on the other hand, options is an agreement which will provide you the rights to purchase or trade the stock at an exact price by an exact date.

An options trading was innate in 1973, so that once an options market developed to a dynamic marketplace. As said by statistics amassed by the Options Industry Council, the entire capacity of option agreements operated on the U.S. exchanges in 2007 was about 3 billion, and it was a record.

The market has subsequently developed through to a classy exchange vehicle. For example, you could predict; several market consultants also some depositors who formed plans and which are known as options trading tactics. The first supposed option purchaser was the Greek mathematician and theorist Thales of Miletus.

For several persons used to through exchange stocks, it might be correct that they are excited to response to the requests. So, what are the options trading? It is the common question for the people. The most important answer of it is that it operated options or choice that always worth your privileges on the stock market. It means a single person takes the rights to the marketplace or else buying individual stock ensuring a particular period and amount range. A call option is that the buyer decides in purchasing securities, though at the time marketing securities and it known as the put option. Therefore, in several circumstances, when other customers apply both of these choices including the similar stock, that keep an eye on the specified date and amount value. It is mostly known as the dual option transaction.

I am sure; you need to know a lot about options trading. If you want to, then you should be aware of the term. Possibly the toughest portion is that how to identify the different conditions. When you catch the opportunity to know this guff which they procedure to change schemes, it would be stress-free to create choices. It permits you to consider directly about the worth of the stocks, uncertainty there are actions to guess. You can choose well on whatever exchange options to the procedure when your information of this particular scheme is sufficient. A wise sample is, once the price of the stock rises, the best choice is to think through a call option. The benefit of it, you will be able to buy the stock at the poorer price as well as sell the stock at the above price in future.

Though this hint is workings, if the price of the stock rises and if not, you can discover it tough to the market. The stocks since they converted unworkable. Once you select the transaction option, you only purchase the stocks and after their actual worth go down. It is a reverse way of a call option. Each of the two options, you need the chance or correct to recompense a quality to the seller. It is while consuming particular exchange methods to obtain the place and stay capable of making benefit.

Option cash is the most skilled dealers demand the fraction; you are giving. It is real, whatever you may lose in the event the stock market changes differing your tactics. Options trading develop beneficial on this condition since you need restriction even uncertainty you're wasting money. For the reason of this, several brokers deliberate the trade options since if you're scared of devoting new funds for your schemes, you need to be coincidental to think through capitalizing slight amount. It simply worth that, you need to acquire to trial once uncertainty you need to use the options trading over get knowledge about the strict policies. If you are self-assured sufficient to follow your plans, this is vital to choose precisely to escape compelling yourself. Currently, you may also learn about the changed expensive exchange software through online. It can also give you advantages to spread your goals.

The benefit of Options is:

1. Better Price Competence
2. A smaller amount of Danger (depend on how purchasers use them)
3. Higher Possibilities of Earnings
4. More Tactical Replacements

There are several kinds of stuff to think while sharing options:

1. You are not beholden to take an action through the options which you are buying. For a wise example, when you are buying options and decide not to do anything through them the options convert valueless when the finishing date of 30 days to some years passes. However, you could misplace hundred percent of your venture in the choice at that idea.

2. Options are usually agreements on the stock otherwise an index and in most circumstances, be contingent on which is the primary advantage of an option. The brokers of the options don't hand over several properties, till the purchaser agrees to go to the options which they have bought.

3. By learning the specific stocks, you are thoughtful of chasing the option on; however, you can relief yourself by escaping damages and valueless options at a period of finishing.

There are also two simple types of options usually available, and they're:

1. The call option is, once a buyer purchases the privileges to an approved upon the amount of an original stock or another benefit from the broker. These usually bought, when the purchaser assumes the stock to increase in worth. It is mandatory for the buyer to take steps on these types of options earlier the choice finishes if it creates economic logic to make sure of consequently.

2. The put option is often the opposite of a call option. In that case, the put option purchaser has a right to vend an advantage at a prearranged value, earlier to the termination of any put options. So, these could usually be bought uncertainty the buyer imagines the stock or another benefit to dropping the price.

There are almost four kinds of members in the options market. It depends on the position the member usually take. The positions are-

1. Purchaser of Calls
2. Brokers of Calls
3. Buyers of Puts
4. Brokers of Puts

Those people who purchase options are known as holders, and those who trade options are known as writers. Moreover, purchasers of calls and puts are assumed to have long positions, but the brokers of calls and puts are considered to have short positions.

There is some essential difference between purchasers and brokers of call and put options. The differences are-

1. Call holders and put holders known as purchasers are not indebted to purchase or vend, they only have the choice to use their rights if they decide to use.
2. Call writers and put writers known as brokers are indebted to purchase or trade. The brokers might be needed to create decent on an undertaken to purchase or trade.

Options exchange may contain a good agreement of danger, after you bought separately, however, if you are well-informed and if you can take classy steps that create the usage of options not as much of dangerous and more satisfying than unpretentious stock obtaining. If the depositor creates the strength required to edify themselves on these following techniques, then they can drive a long way to make a decent salary and reducing their danger.

CHAPTER 1: LEARNING THE LINGO

An option trader is anybody that purchases as well as offers choices within the capital marketplace. A good investor is actually anybody that purchases as well as offers choices within the capital marketplace. Because trading options are most often carried out via on the internet buying and selling agents. It is also often called on the internet trading options or even on the internet choice buying and selling.

Before starting your service as option traders, you will have to know the lingo.

What is lingo?

This is accurate within just about any stroll associated with existence. However, it's especially accurate with regards to buying and selling choices. Along with choices, a few people are associated with conditions to comprehend. A few of these conditions, such as places as well as phone calls, are extremely fundamental and you ought to know about all of them.

A few conditions, nevertheless, need a bit more description. Whenever putting a good choices purchase, you need to be sure that you obtain the text properly. The next "language" can make much more feeling while you have more acquainted with choices. Because choices tend to be therefore flexible as well as because you may be each a choice purchaser as well as a choice vendor, it's essential that you should understand the next conditions:

Fundamental Trading options Conditions

Purchasing to Open -- When you wish to purchase over the phone or perhaps a place choice, you'll be buying phone calls to open or even buying places to open up. You're the purchaser, and also you tend to be buying to open a brand new placement.

Promoting to Near -- Let's state you purchase the phone choice with regard to $3. Throughout the following fourteen days, this rises within worth in order to $5. Therefore, you choose to market your own phone choice (this had been the buy to open). When you wish to market, the actual lingo is selling to near. You purchased something to begin a situation; you're promoting this in order to near away which placement.

Promoting to Open up -- You are able to open up a situation through promoting a choice. Think about this as the choice author or even alongside it from the agreement that's heading to defend me against a good responsibility. In the event that you will create the protected phone, for example, you'd currently personal the actual share. However, to complete your own choice purchase, the actual expression is selling phone calls to open (followed through regardless of the 30 days as well as hit cost may be). In order to open up this particular placement, you're promoting as well as consuming the actual high quality.

Purchasing to Near -- When you attend near away your own protected phone placement, you need to near the actual deal through purchasing back again that which you offered. Therefore, the buy is to close the purchase.

Marketplace Vs Restrict Purchases

The main kinds of purchases (for each share as well as options) tend to be marketplace or even restrict purchases.

The market order indicates a person is prepared to purchase the protection from its presently detailed cost. This is unable to imply your assured cost. Costs can alter, however, usually purchases undergo rapidly that you'll most likely end up receiving the detailed "ask" cost (if you're purchasing, which is). Unless of course, the fundamental share is shifting quickly (thus producing all of the choices relocate lock-step), you'll be stuffed possibly from or even correct around the detailed "ask" or even "offer" cost.

The "limit purchase," however, is exactly where a person state what cost you need to purchase the choice with regard to (or market the possibility with regard to should you currently personal it).

Why make use of restrict purchases? Nicely, for just one, they're excellent resources to make use of whenever you can't hold off your PC the whole day awaiting the best cost to look. Obviously, if you wish to purchase something for any better cost compared to happen to be detailed, you aren't assured of purchasing within from which cost. However because of share cost variances throughout the day, it's incredible the number of occasions you are able to sneak within in a somewhat much better cost, simply because of the choices encounter every single day.

Day as well as GTC Purchases

Just like shares, you have to state a period component for every purchase. Both of the typical purchases tend to be "day orders" and also "good 'til canceled" (GTC) purchases. Along with each purchase, you'll more often than not key in the "day" purchase. In the event that you're prepared to purchase at this time, a person may state each day purchase (then hang in there to ensure you're stuffed upon which trade).

It's not really enjoyable to understand per week later on that you simply in no way purchased within the industry a person believed a person do (especially when the share or even choice is actually upward substantially), therefore it's better to key in day purchases whenever creating jobs.

Halts

An end purchase is definitely a purchase which will get into impact whenever a particular cost is arrived at. This particular seems as being a restricted purchase. It stops the position beneath where the share or even choice happens to be buying and selling.

For instance, you have 10 agreements associated with XYZ Corp. You purchased all of them with regard to $3. forty (or $3, 400). You need to walk out a city, as well as in case XYZ doesn't proceed the proper way (up), you need to bend from this industry in a particular cost as well as restrict your own deficits. This is actually the ideal scenario with regard to putting an end purchase.

Keep in mind, whenever purchasing choices have the built-in cease associated with types. (Therefore you are able to just shed the limited, restricted amount of cash -- how much money this required to purchase the possibility, to begin with. That's the most you are able to shed, and that's why it's a kind of the "stop" purchase.)

However more to the point, if you choose to key in an end purchase that's as well near to the present bid/offer on the specific choice. You could discover yourself halted from the industry sooner than you anticipate (maybe because of a good intra-day slip associated with a few kind). As well as even worse, you may be on a holiday or even for your PC display and never recognize you've already been offered from the industry.

In a case over, you are able to merely location an end from, state, $5. forty ($2 greater than exactly where you have within from $3. forty, but nonetheless around $2 beneath in which the share happens to be buying and selling with regard to from $7. 20) and revel in remaining in the industry. In case your choices visit $8. 20 within worth, you merely proceed your own cease as much as $6. forty.

That you can do trailing stops by hand through working upon every single day as well as modifying your own cease purchases (by carrying out a cancel/replace order). Nevertheless, there are several broker agent systems which will location the actual trailing halts for you personally. You merely let them know what lengths underneath the cost you would like your own cease, as well as it may be carried out for you personally.

Depending Purchases

This is a good purchase that's distinctive to choices. Choices on the share tend to be based on exactly where which share happens to be listed. Within the choices in the world, the share is also known as the "underlying." (In truth, you'll listen to lots of discussing "the underlying" with regards to choices … the actual share is actually exactly what "underlies" the choices)

It means that choices alter within cost since the fundamental share modifications within cost. Choices are associated with the actual share cost. You can state choices on their personal tend to be depending on the fundamental share cost.

As well as that's exactly what the depending purchase is actually. It's merely a method to key in a good purchase to purchase a choice, but rather associated with indicating the possibility cost you would like, a person stipulate exactly where you would like the actual share in order to the industry from prior to your own purchase is activated.

Reason of learning the lingo

Now it is a question, do we need to learn the lingo?

It is a vital question for option traders. It is true that learning the lingo is essential for option traders. It is important because of the following reasons, these are given below:

Reason 1:

In order to be familiar with everything feasible concerning this perform, the professional people should also realize the actual trading policy, each like an occupation so that as a location to operate. Such as each and every occupation, you have to discover the unique language.

Reason 2:

Partially specialized, partially slang, high of its standardized about the English-speaking phase. Like an operating system professional, you have to know about this particular vocabulary, just like the auto technician has to know the titles associated with their resources.

Reason 3:

As your theater instructors, as well as company directors, may wish to talk to a person within the language from the theater when you are focusing on your own class workouts as well as within manufacturing, you're by using this on the internet appendix to go over these types of conditions.

Your own instructor may determine exactly what part of the actual lexicon from the phase you'll need instantly. The rest is going to be set aside for that period when you're really dealing with company directors within manufacturing.

CHAPTER 2:
WHAT MAKES A SKILLFUL OPTIONS TRADER?

An option trader is any person who will buy and also markets options in the capital market. Since options trading will be performed by means of on the web alternative investing brokerages, additionally it is known as on the web options trading or perhaps on the web alternative investing. Alternative investing and also options trading and investing are very different from several ranges.

Inventory dealers acquire if the inventory increases, and also drop any time that decreases.

Nonetheless, options dealers (call and also set quality buyers) not necessarily need to find the proper course with the inventory, nevertheless the stock's shift need to take place inside a moment (before the particular expiry date). Moreover, there exists a quality integrated: the particularly meant volatility (IV): which shows us simply how much some other contact and also set dealers to assume in which inventory to go. As a result, not merely carry out these kinds of speculators will need the particular root to go inside the proper course and also in a specific timeframe.

There are many positive aspects of being able to options trading as a possible purchase method yet several positive aspects will be in which investing options needs one to devote smaller amount money to a purchase when compared to an inventory or some other form of business needs. Through the use of an alternative, you can make the maximum amount of or maybe more income much like other styles regarding investments. Now it is a question, what makes a skillful options trader?

There are lots of paths to being an expert options trader. Whenever monetary companies sponsor with regard to buying and selling jobs, these people have a tendency to consider individuals with levels within mathematics, architectural as well as difficult sciences instead of merely individuals with financial skills. There's also various buying and selling work -- a number of that need client dealing with conversation abilities around graph experienced. Nevertheless, we'll take a look at a few of the abilities which are needed of investors. Now I am going to discuss some major skills in options trading. These are given below:

Analytical Skill

If you wish to be an expert options trader, you'll have to discover and evaluate your personal buying and selling. It's hard, but you will get lots of advantages as a result. To begin with, you are able to enhance your own buying and selling as well as allow it to be much more lucrative. Next, you are able to enhance your own analytical abilities. It is important you will get through buying and selling.

If you want to investigate your own competitors, you may enhance your own analytical abilities. A good investor may evaluate and may discover disadvantages in most of the challenges. You are able to enhance your own analytical considering by utilizing unique buying and selling software program. This kind of software program will help you gather useful details about your own competitors. You'll have to evaluate these details. This will help you earn. The greater a person evaluate your own competitors the greater your own buying and selling.

Options buying and selling can provide a person great analytical considering. This will help you pull findings within hard circumstances whenever you don't have sufficient info. It's a really advantageous ability simply because the existence frequently provides us inadequate details about the problem as well as we must create a hard option. Your own analytical abilities can help you almost everywhere.

Whenever you focus on option buying and selling in the capital market, you are able to enhance your own analytical abilities. Whenever you enhance your own analytical abilities a person begins working on option buying and selling much better.

It is true that an option trader can get a chance to evaluate information rapidly. There's a large amount of mathematics involved with buying and selling, however, it is symbolized via graphs along with indications and designs through specialized evaluation. As a result, investors have to create their own analytical abilities to allow them to identify developments as well as developments within the graphs.

Research

Investors must have a proper desire with regard to info along with a need to discover all of the appropriate information which affects the investments in the capital market. Many investors produce calendars associated with financial produces as well as arranged bulletins which have measurable results about the capital marketplaces. When you are along with these types of info resources, investors can respond to brand new info since the marketplace continues to be processing this.

Indeed, on the internet trading demands just a few clicks; nevertheless, you should not really turn out to be over-zealous. Since you are somewhat taken off the procedure associated with really dealing with your hard earned money, you can easily overlook that certain incorrect click on will set you back 1000s of dollars. Rather, strategies on the internet trading while you might all of your additional expense efforts. The investigation may be crucial to ensure a person makes the most of this particular -- which will give a chance to help to make fast choices.

Focus

The focus is ability also it boosts the more investor's physical exercise this. Simply because there's a lot of monetary info available, investors require every single child develop within about the essential, actionable information which will impact their own deals. A few investors additionally focus within about the kinds of investments these people industry on allowing them to deepen their own knowledge of a particular field, business or even foreign currency to the stage exactly where this gets the aggressive benefit towards much less specific investors.

One main difficulty along with operating your choices buying and selling online businesses is actually distraction! The web is a substantial supply of info and it is common to stroll away from your own goal when you are discovering something on the internet. Trading options aren't any various, you'll probably run into an incredible number of referrals in relation to this particular subject, a few that would end up being really useful, however, the majority is only going to work like a distraction. Remain focused in your job, you are able to usually save additional web pages as well as study all of them later on. Or else you will discover that you have squandered a couple of hours on the internet, examining choices or even info you need to intuitively understand you will not make use of.

Control

Together along with concentrate is actually managed. The investor must manage his / her feelings as well as stay with the buying and selling strategy and technique. This is particularly essential within controlling danger by utilizing cease deficits or even getting earnings from arranged factors. Many methods are made therefore the investor manages to lose just a little within poor deals and methodically increases much more on great deals. Whenever investors begin to obtain psychological regarding their own deals -- great or even poor -- technique is out the actual eye-port.

Because brand new investors start in the actual marketplaces where people frequently discover there's a costly understanding contour towards the monetary marketplaces. The investor that has selected specialized evaluation since the approach to the option may quickly discover it isn't because simple because all the publications and websites allow it to seem. The actual solitary greatest cause is which buying and selling by itself are really a mental online game so when placing real cash at risk, many brand new investors stress and be the actual losers within the online game. Those people who are skilled investors recognize that is the specialized evaluation by itself function. Recognizing designs brought on by group concern or even avarice constitutes the foundation associated with specialized evaluation by itself. Brand new investors have to conquer the feelings associated with concern and avarice when they need to be being prosperous investors prior to going shattered.

Certainly, the brand new investor needs to learn how to control their own feelings. It is easier for truthful skilled investors will acknowledge it's something for these people who have a problem with nonetheless. Here are a few methods for you to learn how to keep the feelings under control:

Perfect buying and selling technique as well as stick to it. Define your own strategy in options trading. Do not begin hearing trading experts as well as their own share recommendations. Avoid the majority of share discussion boards (at minimum before you obtain self-confidence within yourself). Probably the most prosperous investors learn how to believe with regard to on their own and consider individual obligation for his or her buying and selling. Whenever you cease subsequent your own strategy and begin busting your personal guidelines you are most likely buying and selling on feeling.

Don't turn out to be psychologically mounted on your own deals. If you are viewing the buying price of your own share just like a hawk and be elated once the cost rises and stressed out once the cost falls, you are buying and selling upon feeling. Keep in mind, your own buying and selling technique ought to be therefore ingrained that you simply industry just like an automatic robot.

Take sufficient placement dimensions. Do not have a placement dimension bigger than 10 % of the accounts worth. Big placement dimensions are excellent when the cost rises however always remember that the dropping industry associated with too big the dimension may decimate your own buying and selling accounts. This can help maintain concern under control.

Remember, it is OKAY to consider the reduction. For those who have an agenda to reduce deficits, going for a reduction is simply a part of buying and selling. Actually, professionals encounter deficits. The distinction is actually they have an agenda with regard to controlling all of them.

Report Maintaining

Probably essential secrets to buying and selling are reported maintaining. If your investor information the outcomes associated with his / her deals faithfully, after that enhancing is the issue associated with screening as well as tweaking methods to locate a prosperous one. It's difficult to exhibit improvement if you're maintaining precise information.

CHAPTER 3: THE BENEFITS OF OPTIONS TRADING

Despite the fact that Options trading may exist some kind of dangers, it's regarded as the less dangerous method of buying and selling exactly where generating higher come back is extremely quick.

Whilst talking about on the internet buying and selling, the investor is provided the chance to begin buying and selling having a minimal amount of cash associated with $10 based on the buying and selling device selected. The Options trading is decreased since it provides the chance to the investor to get less than he is able to pay for to get rid of. In addition, the broker agent system signifies towards the investors the precise quantity that they have the chance to earn and also the quantity they'll shed, before the expense which created. When the comeback or even the possible reduction conjectures don't match the actual investor, the second option may get the chance to alter their expense to some scaled-down or even higher quantity.

Consequently, options trading provide the chance to investors to judge the actual dangers prior to these people commit their own cash, the industry function which other styles associated with the capital system doesn't supply. Regardless of just how much the capital marketplace techniques, the actual investor will be conscious of their possible deficits.

Investment for online trading

Binary options trading is more popular amongst investors on multiple websites. This particular recognition is a result of the different method of buying and selling they provide. Furthermore, the investors are able to keep track of their own on the internet buying and selling expense through buying and selling how much money they need. By doing this associated with buying and selling allows the absolute minimum expense associated with $10 for each deal, producing the internet deals on economical based on the buying and selling device selected. In addition,

Options trading provides an array of capital property to purchase, for example Foreign exchange, goods, and shares.

- Foreign exchange -- That explains modifications within foreign currency, for example, UNITED STATES DOLLAR, EUR as well as AUD
- Goods -- Alloys, for example, Silver and gold, Essential oil and much more
- Shares -- They are large businesses for example Search engines as well as Apple Company that can be found in the resource checklist.

Quick Results

Nowadays investors interesting on Options trading system, wish to produce higher earnings inside a fairly brief time period. When compared with additional conventional capital buying and selling techniques, trading options creates an extremely quick come back. It provides the chance to possess a revenue border as much as 85% in the preliminary expense created. The expiration occasions on the buying and selling systems are fairly brief with respect to the buying and selling device selected. For instance, while using the Pace Option device, the expiration period generally remain in between 30 to 3 hundred mere seconds. On the other hand, conventional buying and selling are kept with regard to the lengthier time period and it can move up to many years in some instances. The chance to industry quickly on capital marketplaces combined with possible of getting higher results is the majority of appealing function associated with binary trading options. If your investor works for several successful deals, he is able to create a considerable revenue in 2 hours.

Are Options Trading Simple?

It is a million dollars question. Some people believe that it is a simple task. Now it is a question, is it simple? To be able to accelerate the procedure in the preliminary expense towards the first industry, agents possess made certain which buying and selling Options trading are easy as you possibly can. Apart from, you will find a few actions included between your putting your signature on up to and including system phase with selecting the capital resource of the investor which may decide to commit on. Individuals actions likewise incorporate the option from the quantity of the buyer really wants to industry, picking a the resource, he or she really wants to industry along with and also the path he or she believes the marketplace may proceed through the finish from the expiration period. The investor will get via each one of these phases within just a few mouse clicks on options trading software.

In addition, the revenue or even reduction the traders may experience will be based on the variances from the worth from the resource. If your investor thinks the price of the options is increasing, then he will call to his trading center. While when the investor thinks the marketplace is actually slipping, he'd commit on the "put" option. To be able to make sure that the "call" is actually lucrative, the actual shutting cost ought to be more than the actual hit cost in the expiration period. Appropriately, for any "put" to become lucrative, the cost should be the actual hit cost in the expiration period.

Are Options trading easy?

Because the majority of the buying and selling systems are web-based, they may be utilized almost everywhere with no downloading so long as the investor comes with a web connection. This particular accessibility makes it simple for that investor too frequently as well as easily examine their own options and keep track of the capital marketplace on the 24/7. Apart from, since the system provides the use of worldwide marketplaces, investors may continuously maintain buying and selling in the day time. Furthermore, the actual web-based systems are on desktop computer systems in addition to laptop computers, tabs as well as cell phones that boost the buying and selling entry. The mobile software is extremely well-liked and it is suitable for Google android as well as IOS software program.

Buying and selling Options trading may be the new pattern nowadays. This particular developing recognition, as well as notoriety, has remote instances originated from the truth that it's fairly simple to attempt this particular experience which is accessible. To prevent about the incorrect aspect from the street, the investor ought to, to begin with, help to make the comprehensive investigation to be able to pick the most dependable broker agent of the organization. Whilst talking about binary options buying and selling, the option from the company may be the toughest action for 2 factors. The first thing is simple because there's a huge quantity of trading options companies and also the 2nd cause, which is controlled and regards their own guarantee. Consequently, this particular essential option may figure out the entire trip from the investor. As soon as this task carried out, it's recommended regardless of whether you're and skilled investor or even not really to handle a few investigation concerning the capital marketplace and also to make use of the academic resources of the system that you've chosen for you.

Nowadays, more investors are coming to options trading. Many software manufacturers produce Options trading software for potential investors. This particular software program is easy to use, as well as binary trading options (broker) systems make sure this particular to ensure that customers aren't delaying.

All of you need to do forecast if the resource cost goes upward or even lower. This is something possible to discover by yourself through examining the actual capital marketplaces, as well as how you can do that is by using the program which buying and selling systems provide on the internet. Here are some advantages of utilizing binary trading options software program:

- Buying and selling software program offer marketplace info instantly, which makes it simpler that you should help to make proper conjecture generally, therefore reducing the strain or even concern with dropping your own expense.

- The program offers the establishing associated with free of charge demonstration company accounts upon which you'll exercise, once more utilizing real-time marketplace info. Therefore you may make simulated deals and obtain encounter before you decide to really start buying and selling.

- The demonstration accounts additionally allow you to check buying and selling methods. By doing this you are able to learn to make use of numerous confirmed methods and alter a few based on your look, as well as learn how to adjust all of them based on the ever-changing marketplace.

- The program additionally gives you lessons, ideas, discussion boards as well as movies with regard to assistance and assist with your own buying and selling choices. Keep in mind that the majority of agents provide free of charge demonstration company accounts, you will be anticipated to create some kind of repayment to be able to entry the program. When you register as a fellow member, it is possible to obtain the program.

- This particular software may also dual upward like a binary choice indicators supplier, allowing you to acquire information and figure out the actual asset's cost.

To become the prosperous options trading investor, you have to find out how the marketplace functions as well as realize it's developments. Using binary trading options software will help you to improve your own abilities as well as the understanding of binary trading options.

CHAPTER 4: COMMON BEGINNERS MISTAKES

Options are an excellent buying and selling a device that may be found in just about all marketplace problems, possibly to create earnings, or even hedge danger. There are many brand new investors' help to make once the key in the planet associated with trading options. Whenever utilized improperly, may erode your own accounts rapidly, or even within the most detrimental situation produce border phone calls. Listed here are 7 errors newbie options investors help to make, as well as how to prevent all of them.

1. Concentrating on OTM Options

From the cash (OTM) phone or even place options are usually less expensive, a lot of investors look at all of them like a good offer. Whilst this is accurate in some instances, options are listed so that you simply aren't heading to obtain a free of charge lunch time. The high quality, or even worth from the option whenever you purchase this, decays as time passes. Consequently, the cost must not proceed over (for the phone option) or even beneath (put option) your own hit cost, however it requirements to do this prior to the option expires, as well as through sufficient in order to counteract the price of the possibility.

It may be hard to earn money with this particular strategy. Occasionally buying and selling OTM options is really a legitimate technique, however, don't obtain captured within the snare associated with convinced that simply because the possibility is less expensive and it's much better to offer compared to an additional option. Measure the likelihood how the fundamental resource may surpass the hit cost prior to expiration, depending on historic habits, prior to purchasing OTM options.

2. Define a strategy

Options are extremely versatile, as well as may be used in most marketplace problems. Although not just about all option methods work in most marketplace problems. Whenever a good fundamental resource is relaxed as well as hardly shifting, purchasing OTM phone or even place options isn't prone to create great results so long as the fundamental marketplace continues to be toned.

However, composing protected options (when you've got a placement within the fundamental share as well as create options towards it) with this atmosphere may create extra money for you personally. There's also additional methods which are more complicated, for example, Metal Condors, that include getting several jobs as well as creating a revenue in the event that the buying price of the fundamental doesn't proceed a lot. The same as share investors are trained to diversify, options investors also needs to diversify the techniques utilized. Put into action on various techniques for various marketplace problems, as well as with regard to various shares or even property depending on their own habits.

3. Lacking an exit panels

A significant mistake with regard to brand new option investors in most marketplaces really isn't getting a good exit panel. Whenever you have an industry you're looking to earn money, however how much cash? Exactly how are you going to choose the quantity of revenue that's suitable? In the event that this appears like your own option will end useless would your market to recover a few of the price, lowering your reduction? Are you going to contain the option till expiration?

Observe four Methods to Leave the Dropping Industry

They are queries which have to be tackled prior to the industry. Produce an arrangement for such a practical revenue focus on is actually, in line with the historic motion from the fundamental resource. Figure out how you'll reduce the danger, so you'll leave the industry if it's dropping as well as appears like this won't complete within the cash.

4. Unaware to promote Shifting Occasions

State a person produce a good options industry depending on peaceful marketplace situation, as well as you'll revenue so long as the fundamental resource remains docile. You'll wish to determine in the event that any kind of marketplace shifting occasions tend to be because of away within the share in the period body of the industry. A good income discharge, for instance, might toss the wrench inside your strategy, growing volatility, altering marketplace problems and placing your own "quiet times" technique needlessly at risk.

Be familiar with what's occurring within the marketplaces you're buying and selling. Main financial occasions for example given min's or even a good income discharge can alter marketplace problems rapidly, as well as your technique ought to support for your options trading. Keep track of the financial diary with income diary and produce an arrangement for the way you may industry close to main information occasions. You may choose the industry near to these types of occasions, therefore getting rid of the large unfamiliar associated with the way of the marketplace may respond to the big event.

5. Disregarding Constant Increases

Creating a large obtain on the industry is really a good sensation, however, it's also difficult to do. Within hindsight you can easily place the house operates deals, however, in real-time, it's also harder. Most of the time shares perform absolutely nothing (or absolutely nothing major), also it isn't simple to determine whenever one of these is all about to increase.

However, marketplaces continuously proceed a number of portion factors inside an issue associated with times. Consequently, producing constant scaled-down results could be simpler compared to producing one large comeback. Whilst producing 2% per week depending on a regular technique isn't because attractive like a 20% come back, you'll most likely have the ability to stand upward several 2% days prior to actually recording a large champion.

Additionally, keep in mind that each time a person create a little, as well as constant, obtain you're creating your own funds. This particular creates compounding results. However, each time a person shed on the "home run" industry you're decreasing funds, decreasing the quantity of funds readily available for deals. With time it's an extremely damaging impact since it gets tougher as well as tougher I to recover deficits because placement dimensions reduce of decreasing funds.

6. Attempting to "Time" Legged Deals

Option methods frequently need getting several options jobs simultaneously. This kind of deals needs a number of dealings, which ought to happen simultaneously to achieve the required placement. A few investors can make the actual dealings individually although, trying to improve their own revenue somewhat through obtaining one option with an uptick as well as an additional on the downtick, for instance. The issue is that you might wind up lacking your own eye-port to determine the positioning. When the cost starts to operate before you decide to establish your own jobs you might be remaining subjected to unfamiliar danger.

In the event that you're developing a placement that needs several option deals, consider all of them all at one time. Don't attempt to choose your own admittance factors. Even though this functions it'll just possess a minimal impact on general success, and may screw up the initial technique when the cost techniques towards a person when you are waiting for a much better admittance.

7. Not Addressing Created Options

Composing options is a method to generate profits, while you have the high quality through promoting the possibility in advance; when the option expires useless you're able to keep your whole quantity obtained.

The high quality may be the optimum revenue although, and when the fundamental resource will go towards a person, a person possibly encounter big deficits (this is the reason why the majority of option authors possess a placement within the fundamental resource too, known as protected option writing). The error from the option author is faltering to secure a few of the high quality once they possess the opportunity.

In the event, you marketed alternatives with $2. 00 and will escape the particular business if the quality will be $0. 45 meaning an individual nonetheless arrive at retain 80% with the authentic quality an individual acquired (fewer commissions): an individual nonetheless pants pocket $1. 58 multiplied simply by how many explains to you regarding explains to you an individual published alternatives about. Preserving 80% surpasses probably being forced to pay above funds (or the inventory in the event the alternative will be covered) in the event the value should go in opposition to an individual just before expiry.

The underside Collection

Options really are an excellent device, functional in the most marketplace problems; however, they may be devastating if your investor doesn't learn how to put into action on these types of monetary devices correctly. Diversify your own methods as well as get ready for possible modifications within marketplace problems which may be powered through main information occasions. Understand how you'll leave deals, as well as concentrate on constant results more than house operates deals. In case your placement demands several option deals, perform all of them simultaneously; faltering to do this might endanger the actual technique. Whenever you create options, don't hesitate to leave the actual industry as well as maintain the main high quality, particularly when there is the query regarding if the option may end useless or even not really.

CHAPTER 5: THE PRINCIPLES OF PRICING

Traders may use options to obtain earnings through non-dividend-paying shares to buy a share as well as restrict for its danger. Investors may use options to include influence by having a suitable degree of danger that's genuinely restricted, in addition to industry upward, lower as well as range-bound marketplaces.

In spite of these types of advantages as well as constantly developing quantity (more compared to 15% substance quantity development because 1973), options continue to be within their childhood concerning open public knowing as well as popularity.

Listed here are 10 crucial concepts which beginners to options ought to bear in mind because they make plan for the options industry. Now I am going to discuss these concepts.

Concept 1

Understand the distinction in between utilizing options to get as well as utilizing options to industry: Traders concentrate on the advantages of long-term share possession, and they ought to make use of options to purchase, market, or even safeguard share jobs, in order to improve earnings through share jobs. Think about a good buyer likely to purchase share whenever he or she gets the year-end reward. This particular buyer can purchase 1 phone these days for every 100 gives he or she programs to buy. The phone option is really an agreement that provides the customer to purchase the fundamental share in the hit cost any time before termination day. Basically, it is with regard to having to pay the price of the shares for these days. When the share cost is greater once the buyer gets the actual reward, he then nevertheless can buy the planned-for quantity of gives. With no phone, the amount of gives would need to end up being decreased provided the larger share cost.

Investors, as opposed to traders, tend to be short-term marketplace timers along with small curiosity about having the fundamental share, and they frequently make use of a higher level of influence. Bought options provide investors the possibility of substantial influence along with restricted danger. However, the danger is real. Options may shed 50% or even more of the cost very quickly in the event that the buying prices of the fundamental share techniques the wrong manner. Additionally, out-of-the-money options end useless from termination for any complete lack of the cost compensated, in addition, profits.

Concept 2

Traders, that make use of options require a strategy: May the bought option end up being worked out or even offered if it's in-the-money from termination? Protected authors have to know whether they are prepared to market the fundamental share. Otherwise, it is advisable to choose ahead of time from exactly what cost the phone call is going to be repurchased or even folded to an additional option.

Concept 3

Know how as well as the reason why option costs later: Option costs later in a different way compared to share costs, therefore option investors have to strategy in a different way compared to share investors. An average problem through beginners to options is real: "The share proceeded to go upward, however, my personal phone didn't! Focusing on how costs alter is important to utilizing options effectively.

The worth associated with time provides theoretical ideals of the 50-strike phone from various share costs and various times to termination provided the mentioned presumptions regarding rates of interest, returns as well as volatility. Each one of the series within the desk is really a various share cost, as well as each one of the posts is really a various quantity of times to termination. This discloses 2 essential ideas regarding option costs -- the idea of "delta" which associated with "non-linear period rot.

The idea of "delta" is which for any $1 alter within the fundamental share cost, the worthiness of the phone can change through under $1. Within "The worth of your time, when the share cost increases through $50 to $51 from 3 months, the $50 increases through 50¢. Delta explains the anticipated alter within an option's cost for any $1 alter within the fundamental stock's cost, which means this is referred to as using a delta associated with 0.50.

The desk demonstrates which option costs don't reduce at the exact same price after a while to termination, presuming elements besides time for you to termination stay continuous. Think about the middle strip where the share is $50. Because the time for you to termination reduces through 50% through 3 months to forty-five times, the worthiness from the $50 phone reduces through around 31% through $3.20 in order to $2. Twenty-five. It's this that "non-linear period erosion" indicates.

Searching throughout any kind of strip, you will see how the reduction in the passing of your time, so-called period erosion or even theta, differs based on regardless of whether an option is in-the-money, at-the-money or even out-of-the-money.

Concept 4

Option investors require self-discipline within getting earnings as well as deficits: Very first, possess a revenue focus on as well as near or even decrease how big a situation in the event that which cost is actually arrived at. 2nd, possess a stop-loss stage as well as near or even decrease how big a situation from which cost. 3rd, possess a time period limit as well as near or even decrease how big a situation in the event that nor the actual revenue focus on neither the stop-loss stage tends to be arrived at through the finish of times time period.

Concept 5

Don't get freaked away through volatility: Conceptually, options act like insurance coverage, and also the volatility element in options refers towards the danger element in insurance coverage. It's a key point, however, it's not the only real element. Whilst the idea of volatility isn't without effort apparent in order to beginners, it may be discovered in the event that the first is individual.

Concept 6

It possesses practical anticipation: Learning the actual ideas associated with delta as well as theta (time decay) is definitely an essential action towards the aim of building practical anticipation about how exactly option costs may as well as may not alter as well as just how much revenue possible as well as danger every technique offers.

Concept 7

Buying undervalued options as well as selling over-valued options aren't adequate methods: "Value" is really a very subjective dedication that each investor should help to make separately. Option investors should concentrate on their own three-part predict around or even more compared to "value" of the option.

Concept 8

Selling options" isn't a much better technique compared to "buying options": It's a fantasy which 80-90% associated with options end useless. Around 1 / 3, or even 33%, associated with options end useless whilst 10-15% tend to be worked out. The remainder will be shut just before termination. Whilst option composing (selling) could be a prosperous technique, beginners frequently misunderstand this. There's a cause, there's a high quality to take upon much more danger. There isn't any solution to it -- option purchasers spend reasonably limited associated with described danger as well as option retailers get a high quality to take on danger.

Concept 9

Influence is really a double-edged blade: Option investors ought to handle their own funds in a different way compared to share investors. Your decision is to buy two hundred gives off the trading from $50 for each reveal is extremely various how the option to buy 100 phone trading options from $1 every, despite the fact that each deal includes a good expense associated with $10, 000, excluding profits. Usually, options investors may commit an inferior part of complete funds to every industry. Option investors, nevertheless, may have much more open up jobs compared to share investors.

Concept 10

Create a marketplace predicting method through beginning little, recognizing earnings with deficits as well as through operating at a constant speed: Investors will be able to clarify their own trade-selection procedure inside a couple of phrases. New people can deal which have just little possible earnings as well as deficits, simply because this can improve their own likelihood of sustaining objectivity. Deals should be started and shut to ensure that the trading rhythm is created.

Almost any person may learn how to work on options trading when they invest a couple of hours in each week on their own method. However, you may invest many years without having learning options. Discover these types of concepts as well as go one action at any given time. Options tend to be such as levels of the red onion -- there's always something a new comer to discover. Don't grow to become discouraged as well as, more to the point, don't turn out to be more than assured and believe you realize everything simply because you will get burnt.

CHAPTER 6: OPTIONS TRADING STRATEGIES FOR BEGINNERS

Share investment, options trading, as well as foreign currency buying and selling -- they are a few of the well-liked methods for producing extra earnings apart from selecting the standard methods. Now it is a question, what types of methods we will choose.

Therefore you are currently acquainted with share investment as well as options trading. You do not think of attempting all of them however you'd be happy to understand some possible causes of investment earnings. And thus, your own desire is my personal order! A person arrived right here simply because you need to understand a few information about Options trading. This short article will not make you a specialist about them, however, it can easily provide you a solution of the easiest queries you have now. You don't need to defeat your own minds away!

Foreign currencies are essential to many people in some other part of the world. They're required to operate international companies. For instance, you're a visitor from the United States and want to vacation in European countries. Obviously, you can't spend a large amount of money to visit the most popular holiday destinations presently there. You will have to trade your dollars for that nearby foreign currency.

This is why there's constant have to trade foreign currencies. For this reason truth, Currency markets are just about the greatest capital marketplace in the world.

A few Benefits of Options trading

Therefore, you are able to obtain earnings. Exactly what is to otherwise? Why is this kind of buying and selling much better for a person?

You can test a totally free demonstration accounts

This really is good for the new person as if you're a little uncertain regarding yourself. Attempting a totally free demonstration accounts prepares a person for that period which you will have to commit your hard earned money within the expectations of getting actual earnings. It can help you determine in the event that options trading is perfect for a person.

The marketplace deals twenty-four hours in a day

Therefore, you do not intend to get it done full-time. That is simply good. You are able to do it anytime from the day time since the marketplace in no way sleeps.

There is not any fixed dimension

Wish to take part having a great deal dimension, let's imagine, $25? Not a problem! A person figures out your personal placement dimension.

Presently there you have this; the actual group of fundamental bits of details about options trading. Would you like to check it out? Or even would you like to find out more comprehensive details? A person should pick the second option for the time being. There are many points you should know, and you ought to take advantage of your assets. Certainly, you have to be careful within attempting to invest. It will pay to become daring sufficient to consider dangers. Simply be sure you include sufficient understanding of exactly what you are performing.

You need to attempt your own hands from binary trading options. Within options trading, you won't work as the participant, however, a good buyer spends the cash inside a strong task to generate. That's the reason binary trading options methods are your primary tool. There's a large group of this kind of methods, if you wish to be successful, you have to positively discover as well as utilize those that you prefer and appear guaranteeing. Try to follow the instruction along with easy options trading techniques for newcomers. It ought to be remembered which options trading is the main huge as well as the complex system -- the actual capital marketplace, that is not really disorderly as well as arbitrary, however, the Options trading market works based on particular regulations. Now I am going to discuss some strategies for Options trading for newcomers, these techniques are given below:

Diversity Technique

Caused by the possibility is determined by the overall scenario on the market and also the particular present cost for any specific resource. Just by making use of particular binary trading options technique, an investor may industry effectively and thus, generate upon their opportunities.

Keep in mind that any kind of technique, actually apparently win-win, can't work preferably constantly. Losing can be done and you will generate losses, however, more to the point, don't shed all at one time. Permitting the chance associated with episodic subsidence associated with funds, you shouldn't place all of the cash into 1 option. It's very dangerous as well as careless. Preferably, you ought to have the money, a minimum of 10 investments. This type of sensible as well as the wise mindset is in the direction of down payment known as money diversity. Allow the thought of diversity never simply leaves the mind.

5 Minutes Technique

This tactic is simple, might state actually a good primary easy, which is well suited for newbies who've absolutely no encounter, absolutely no severe funds upon down payment. It doesn't assure 100 % associated with achievement, however, it's likelihood, based on traditional estimations, is near to 80 %. Throughout the day, you should use this frequently, growing, therefore, your own little funds unless of course, obviously, you're very sensible, as well as best of luck won't change from a person.

5 Min's technique is dependent on the truth that many agents permit you to purchase options on the severe degree -- within 5 min's prior to the termination. All that's necessary would be to rummage around the property on the market in order to find one which is actually steady and developing for a long period or even, on the other hand, reduces. Remember to find it's optimum worth, that, without a doubt, this time around can be a switching stage for that pattern, as well as arrived at the historical higher, the pattern most likely can change the movement towards the reverse.

Martingale

The actual theory from the Martingale is actually regarded as much less dangerous and secure whenever buying and selling options trading. Martingale theory is dependent on doubling the next quantities when the prior industry is unsuccessful. That's, should you shed $100, you need to industry once again along with some $200. Should you shed $200, it's the period simply to place $400. You need to your own buying and selling quantity if you earn, or else all of the prior deals to show the really substantial reduction.

Martingale and Kelly Theory

Consequently, to use the actual theory associated with Martingale within its finest type, depending on good fortune, is extremely dangerous. You need to discover the foreign currency set, having a cleanup or even lower pattern associated with cost motion. It's reasonable to presume this pattern won't alter soon. You need to use this particular short-term balance. It's much more dependable to options trading through Martingale theory utilizing binary option indications. Options trading indicators currently provide you with an opportunity to earn, as well as while using theory associated with Martingale you'll significantly improve this.

Quarter-hour Technique

You need to monitor a good resource on quarter-hour time-frame, in the event that all of us observe 3 or even more consecutive candle lights from the exact same color, let's await the rollback. We ought to purchase binary option following two min's dreaming about moving back again. For instance, all of us observe 3 whitened candle lights shut, brand new candlestick starts also it gets into the alternative path -- the cost reduces. All of us wait around 2 min's to create and repair it folded back again.

Triangle

Triangles will vary, however they display the impending discovery cost. The number of items is increasing, portend the impending improve within costs along with a split up, however slipping triangles, on the other hand, tend to be harbingers associated with its most likely drop. Appropriately, investors need to improve or even loss of the cost whenever you observe the actual graph offers created the actual related determine. To determine this, industry ought to aesthetically pull 2 outlines with the factors associated with the opposition as well as assistance. Opposition collection (higher) should be horizontally and assistance collection is situated from a good position. It's apparent which inside a downtrend, investors possess to consider the downwards triangle. Within climbing down triangle, assistance collection is horizontal, opposition collection got rid of from a good severe position into it -- on optimum factors.

CONCLUSION

Nowadays, many investors' portfolios consist of opportunities, for example, shared money, shares as well as provides. However, all of the investments you've available don't finish presently there. Another kind of protection, known as an option, provides a global associated with the chance to advanced traders.

The ability associated with options is based on their own flexibility. These people allow you to adjust or even change your situation based on any kind of scenario which occurs. Options are often as risky or even because traditional while you would like. What this means is that you can do from safeguarding a situation from the decrease to downright wagering about the motion of the marketplace or even catalog.

This particular flexibility, nevertheless, doesn't arrive without having its expenses. Options are complicated investments as well as can be dangerous.

Options include dangers and therefore are not really ideal for everybody. Options buying and selling could be risky within character as well as have considerable danger associated with reduction. Just commit along with danger funds.

In spite of exactly what anyone lets you know, option buying and selling entail danger, particularly if you do not understand what you do. Due to this, lots of people recommend a person avoid options as well as overlook their own living.

However, becoming uninformed associated with any kind of expense locations inside a fragile placement. Probably the risky character associated with options does not match your look. Not a problem -- after that do not theorize within options. However, before you decide to choose not really to purchase options, you need to realize all of them. Not really understanding exactly how options perform is really as harmful because leaping correct within: without having the understanding regarding options you'd not just lose getting an additional product inside your trading toolkit but additionally shed understanding to the operation associated with a few of the planet's biggest companies. Now it is your decision to think about it.